If you could look into the invisible world, you'd see that when the Word of God is spoken, when the promises of God are activated in your life, all hell gets out of the way. This book will make you invincible!

—SID ROTH
HOST, *IT'S SUPERNATURAL!*

I have known Mike Shreve for over thirty years. This book is a life changer! I highly recommend it!

—ROBERT D'ANDREA
PRESIDENT, CHRISTIAN TELEVISION NETWORK

Today we live in the most distracted and disrupted culture in history. The idea of "truth" is laughed at on TV talk shows, and moral principles drift and change with each generation. That's why Mike Shreve's new book, *25 Powerful Promises From God*, is so important at this cultural moment. More than ever we need promises we can depend on and build our lives around. Mike reminds us that God is the author of truth and His promises can be counted on now and forever. In the confusion of a world that can't decide right and wrong, this is a book to keep at the ready. Get it. Read it. Never forget the power and the promises of the God we serve.

—PHIL COOKE, PHD
FILMMAKER, MEDIA CONSULTANT, AUTHOR OF *THE WAY BACK: HOW CHRISTIANS BLEW OUR CREDIBILITY AND HOW WE GET IT BACK*

25
POWERFUL
PROMISES
from
GOD

25
POWERFUL
PROMISES
from
GOD

MIKE SHREVE

CHARISMA
HOUSE

Most CHARISMA HOUSE BOOK GROUP products are available at special quantity discounts for bulk purchase for sales promotions, premiums, fund-raising, and educational needs. For details, write Charisma House Book Group, 600 Rinehart Road, Lake Mary, Florida 32746, or telephone (407) 333-0600.

25 POWERFUL PROMISES FROM GOD by Mike Shreve
Published by Charisma House
Charisma Media/Charisma House Book Group
600 Rinehart Road
Lake Mary, Florida 32746
www.charismahouse.com

Visit the author's website at shreveministries.org.

Library of Congress Cataloging-in-Publication Data:
Names: Shreve, Mike, author.
Title: 25 powerful promises from God / Mike Shreve.
Other titles: Twenty-five powerful promises from God
Description: Lake Mary : Charisma House, 2018. | Includes bibliographical references.
Identifiers: LCCN 2018009069 (print) | LCCN 2018013345 (ebook) | ISBN 9781629995205 (e-book) | ISBN 9781629995199 (trade paper)
Subjects: LCSH: God (Christianity)--Promises.
Classification: LCC BT180.P7 (ebook) | LCC BT180.P7 S53 2018 (print) | DDC
    231.7--dc23
LC record available at https://lccn.loc.gov/2018009069

While the author has made every effort to provide accurate internet addresses at the time of publication, neither the publisher nor the author assumes any responsibility for errors or for changes that occur after publication. Further, the publisher does not have any control over and does not assume any responsibility for author or third-party websites or their content.

18 19 20 21 22 — 987654321
Printed in the United States of America

I dedicate this book to the most loyal, trustworthy, and self-sacrificing person I know: my wife, Elizabeth. She has kept her promises to God, to me, to our children, and to others— which at times has required great personal sacrifice. I have always admired that Christlike quality in her.

God never made a promise that was too good to be true.[1]

—**D. L. Moody**

CONTENTS

FOREWORD

I GREW UP SCHAMBACH. Early in life I was exposed to the hard places of our world, be they in the inner cities of our nation or the third-world nations of our globe. Everywhere we went, we met people who were overwhelmed with poverty, sickness, family brokenness, drug habits, and prostitution. We also met struggling believers, many of whom were fighting off depression and oppression and had to combat the spiritual wickedness surrounding those issues.

Yet in those hard places I saw firsthand the power of the proclamation of the promises of God. My father was a power preacher, but the power was not in his voice or in his delivery; the power was in the Word of God he preached and the gift of faith that brought home the truth of every promise written for healing, financial breakthrough, restoration, and deliverance.

As he would begin to sing, testify, or preach the promises, I could literally feel faith rising from the people. This is the catalyst for renewal and revival. The promises of God and the testimonies of God's people who received the fulfillment of them are sources of hope for the unbeliever. The hope and faith that declaring the promises of God would produce caused thousands to answer the altar calls every night under the great gospel tent.

This book, 25 Powerful Promises From God by Mike Shreve, can be the catalyst for your own faith renewal—your personal revival. I believe the Holy Spirit has a daily message for you on every page. I know how He works; as you read, the scripture will be just what you need to rejoice a little louder and trust God a little more deeply.

As you probably sense, this is not a one-time read. This book is one to keep by your devotional table and chair. You will want quick and easy access to the reminders of all the ways God has supernaturally provided for your health and well-being and for that of your family.

I am sure you will also find that the way the book is formatted will be a powerful ministry tool for you as you encourage your friends and loved ones. Nothing is as powerful as the Word of God. Why give advice when you can give a tried-and-true promise of God, right from His very mouth?

Thank you, Mike, for another very practical, very important book, designed to encourage believers to be everything God intended. I am sure that every reader will be uplifted and challenged to rise higher in the high calling of Christ Jesus.

—DONNA J. SCHAMBACH
EVANGELIST, SCHAMBACH MINISTRIES AND FOUNDATION
WWW.SCHAMBACH.ORG

(Note from author, Mike Shreve: Donna Schambach is the daughter of R. W. Schambach, the evangelist known worldwide for his powerful, faith-building messages and ministry. After I became a Christian, in the fall of 1970, I listened to

Brother Schambach on the radio as often as possible. Years later I was blessed to work with him in some ministry outreaches. His teaching helped to awaken faith for the miraculous in me. It is a great blessing to see Donna carrying on such a faith-filled, Jesus-exalting, world-impacting legacy.)

ESTABLISHING THE REVELATION

For all the promises of God in Him are "Yes," and in Him "Amen," to the glory of God through us.

—2 Corinthians 1:20

CHAPTER 1

PROMISES, PROMISES—
AND ALL OF THEM TRUE!

THERE ARE 7,487 promises in the Bible—sacred pledges God has made to His sons and daughters.[1] Compare that with 31,173 verses in the Bible (or close to it—opinions vary). When you work out the math, you'll discover that about one-fourth of the Bible consists of commitments God has made to His people. Of course, that figure can't be exact because one verse may contain several promises, and another verse may contain none—but still, the comparison is enlightening.

Evidently one of the main reasons the Bible exists is to convey to God's people those divine assurances that empower them to be overcomers in every situation.

Here's a daring statement: true believers will never, I repeat, never—put that word in capital letters in your mind and underline it—<u>NEVER</u> face any situation in life where God hasn't already, in advance, given them a promise powerful enough to push them through the opposition to sure victory on the other side.

Consider these examples:

+ Are you depressed? Here's a promise: "The joy of the LORD is your strength" (Neh. 8:10).

3

+ Do you feel weak? Here's a promise: "He gives power to the faint, and to those who have no might He increases strength" (Isa. 40:29).

+ Do you struggle with doubts? Here's a promise: "Let us look to Jesus, the author and finisher of our faith" (Heb. 12:2).

+ Are you battling sickness? Here's a promise: "The prayer of faith will save the sick, and the Lord will raise him up" (James 5:15).

+ Are you financially strapped? Here's a promise: "You shall remember the Lord your God, for it is He who gives you power to get wealth" (Deut. 8:18, nkjv).

+ Are you thinking God will give up on you? Here's a promise: "He has said: 'I will never leave you, nor forsake you'" (Heb. 13:5).

+ Are you afraid of death? Here's a promise, from the lips of Jesus Himself: "I am the resurrection and the life. He who believes in Me, though he may die, yet shall he live" (John 11:25).

By now you should be convinced. No matter what the negative problem is, there is going to be a positive promise somewhere in the Bible to cancel it, conquer it, and lift you up above it. Most people remind God of their *problems* when they pray; men and women of faith remind God of His *promises*.

One of my favorites, suitable for almost every situation, is 1 John 5:4: "Whoever is born of God overcomes the world, and the victory that overcomes the world is our faith." You might call this scripture "the old one-two" strategy (two calculated punches intended to knock out an opponent).

Right now you may feel as if you're in a boxing ring and your adversary is looming over you with an intimidating glare (the world with all its darkness, pain, and damaging influence). Yet you boldly declare, "I'm born again!" (a heavy-handed punch to the gut). Then twice as loud you shout, "I have faith in the risen Savior and the Word of God!" (a knockout smash to the head). Your opponent crumbles to the mat in front of you, down for the count. The referee is holding up your hand, announcing that you are the winner of the grand trophy.

Can you hear the "great cloud of witnesses" in heaven's grandstands roaring out approval (Heb. 12:1)? When they were here, they had to fight the same enemies, but they learned how to win—against all odds.

Many have called the eleventh chapter of Hebrews "faith's Hall of Fame." It identifies over a dozen men and women of the Bible who overcame great adversities and challenges simply because "through faith" they "obtained promises" (Heb. 11:33).

Now it's your turn.

Will we be able to examine all 7,487 promises in this book? No; that would be impossible. But we will pan for gold. Many books have been written on the general subject of the promises of God, covering a lot of basic territory. This book will focus on the promises that identify the most exceptional supernatural and miraculous aspects of our inheritance.

Are you ready? Do you feel the spiritual adrenaline pumping through your veins? Yes, I can almost hear you whispering, "This book is really going to change my life."

You might want to change that wording slightly. It's not just going to change *your life*. It's going to change *you*—in an excellent and permanent way.

CHAPTER 2

THE MYSTERY OF THE RAINBOW

MY FATHER WAS in the Naval Air Forces. He belonged to a select group called the Hurricane Squadron, a group of gutsy pilots who flew prop planes into the eyes of hurricanes to take weather measurements. (Yes, they had "the right stuff.") I always admired the raw courage it must have taken to do something that daring.

One day when I was still a child, we were looking up at a rainbow, and Dad happened to mention, "When you get up high enough in the atmosphere and look down on a rainbow, it's not always a semicircle—it's often a complete circle." That was a *wow* moment for me—an insight that resurfaced every time I saw one of those amazing "bridges of hope" stretched across the sky.

At first I didn't catch the biblical connection; it was just an intriguing marvel of nature. After I entered into a relationship with God, though, the symbolism impacted me even more. You see, in Scripture a rainbow represents the promises of God. From our earthly perspective we only see the promises themselves, but from a heavenly perspective God sees both His promises and their fulfillment as one and the same thing. If He gives a promise, He intends for it to come to pass.

Let me remind you how it started.

A horrifying, cataclysmic event had just taken place—the global flood, foretold by God, that destroyed every living thing. Only Noah, his family, and the animals in the ark survived (and all the sea creatures that remained). After the waters subsided, Noah exited the ark. With great gratitude, he offered burnt offerings to God, and God responded.

> As for Me, I establish My covenant with you, and with your descendants after you....I have set my rainbow in the cloud, and it shall be a sign of a covenant between Me and the earth. When I bring a cloud over the earth, the rainbow will be seen in the cloud; then I will remember My covenant, which is between Me and you...and the waters will never again become a flood to destroy all flesh.
>
> —GENESIS 9:9, 13–15

It's been thousands of years now, and God has kept His word. The entire world has never been destroyed again by water—and it never will be. How can I be so sure? Because God promised, and because He made a covenant (which is a binding agreement between God and His people).

There have been nine major pacts such as this revealed by God since the beginning of creation. The Scripture calls them "covenants of promise" (because each covenant contained unique promises, relevant to that time, that empowered God's people to live victoriously during their journey through this world). Right now we are living in the era of the new covenant, which is described as "a better covenant...established on better promises" (Heb. 8:6).

Many of these new covenant promises will be unveiled in the chapters ahead.

The nine main covenants God has established are the covenant of creation (made with Adam and Eve in the perfection of paradise), the covenant of redemption (made with Adam and Eve after the fall), the covenant with Noah, the covenant with Abraham, the covenant with Moses, the covenant with the children of Israel in the wilderness, the covenant with David, the new covenant, and the everlasting covenant.

Appropriately, in the last book of the Bible—the climax of this grand story of redemption—we read John's amazing description of the uppermost chamber of the King of kings and Lord of lords:

> There was a throne set in heaven with One sitting on the throne! And He who sat there appeared like a jasper and a sardius stone. *There was a rainbow around the throne*, appearing like an emerald.
>
> —Revelation 4:2–3, emphasis added

Did you catch that? The rainbow is not just *over* God's throne (a semicircle); the rainbow is *around* God's throne (a full circle). Once again, in an ultimate way God is symbolizing that the promises and their fulfillment are one (especially those John was about to encounter in the intense, apocalyptic visions he received).

As you go through this book, try to look at every promise that way—like a full, round rainbow—and praise God as if the fulfillment of that promise is just as sure as the commitment God made.

CHAPTER 3

PATRIARCH OF THE PROMISES

WHEN GOD DECIDES to show up on the doorstep of your life, He arrives with a treasure chest full of promises. Sometimes the promises are from His written Word (the *logos*). At other times they are direct communications to you personally, something called the living word (the *rhema*).

It happened the latter way for a man named Abraham. When God revealed Himself to this great patriarch thousands of years ago, He gave him a series of promises so remarkable and far-reaching that a series of supernatural miracles, signs, and wonders was necessary to bring them all to pass. (See Genesis 12–22.) Here are the primary ones:

+ **Promised offspring:** Abraham and his wife, Sarah, were childless, but God promised that their descendants would be as numerous as the stars, the sand, and the dust of the earth. (See Genesis 13:16; 22:17.) That took a miracle!

+ **Promised global impact:** God pledged to bless Abraham, make his name great, and make him a blessing—so that ultimately, through his seed, all nations and families of the earth would be blessed. (See Genesis 12:1–3; 26:4.) That must have been mind-boggling to him.

+ **Promised deliverance:** God revealed to Abraham that his offspring would spend four hundred years in bondage, but He assured Abraham that He would bring them out with "great possessions" (Gen. 15:14). The way that happened still leaves me awestruck.

+ **Promised land:** God told Abraham his offspring would possess the land inhabited by the Canaanite tribes. It would later appropriately be called "the land of promise" (Heb. 11:9, NKJV). Apparently God also recognizes the importance of *location, location, location.*

+ **Promised ultimate victory:** Finally God promised that the descendants of Abraham would "possess the gate of their enemies" (Gen. 22:17). Foundationally this was fulfilled when the Canaanite cities fell before Joshua, like the walls of Jericho collapsing at the sound of the Israelites shouting the praises of God. On an ultimate level this was speaking of Jesus (the promised seed of Abraham) possessing the "gates of Hades" (the gates of death) for Himself and for all who trust in Him (Matt. 16:18).

These were not Abraham's ideas; these were God's ideas. This great patriarch simply believed what God showed him. The following passage, which describes Abraham's reaction, is one you should memorize.

He staggered not at the promise of God through unbelief; but was strong in faith, giving glory to God; and
being fully persuaded that, what he had promised, he
was able also to perform.
                                    —Romans 4:20–21, kjv

God still communicates to ordinary people extraordinary promises that require miracles, signs, and wonders
to come to pass. Can you imagine what it was like to be
Abraham, to hear such incredible things from God, and
when there was no physical evidence of their fulfillment, to
be bold enough to believe and act on your faith? I love the
following passage.

By faith he lived *in the land of promise* as a stranger,
dwelling in tents with Isaac and Jacob, the *heirs of the
same promise* with him. For he looked for a city which
has foundations, whose builder and maker is God.
                    —Hebrews 11:9–10, mkjv, emphasis added

In other words, Abraham walked through the land God
had promised him as if it belonged to him—because prophetically it did. He drove down stakes and raised his tents.
A small start? Yes, extremely small—but it was a start.
It would take hundreds of years before "the time of the
promise drew near" and God's Word started fully manifesting (Acts 7:17). However, Abraham dared to act as if the
promises were already in motion in his day (because they
were). That's the mind-set you and I need to cultivate too.

If it worked for Abraham, it will work for you. Take
some steps in the direction of your promises. Put down

stakes. Raise your tent. Live there every day. Even before your promises manifest, treat them as if they're already in motion (because they are). Make them your daily confession. Then watch God unfold His plan, one step at a time.

THE CHURCH MOVED BY THE HAND OF GOD

About twenty years ago a worship leader who worked with me shared an amazing and unforgettable story about a church his uncle had pastored—Providence United Methodist Church in Swan Quarter, North Carolina. What happened in the establishment of that church was miraculous. In that region especially, people even refer to it as "The Church Moved by the Hand of God."[1]

In 1874 a group of believers in that quaint waterfront community decided to build a church. They felt impressed to place it on prime property downtown, a lot owned by a man named Samuel Sadler. Unfortunately Mr. Sadler had other plans and refused to sell them the property. Reluctantly they raised their structure at a different location. Then divine intervention took place in a most unexpected way. A hurricane swept up the coast, and about five feet of water surged through the city. The historical account, verified on the Snopes website, reads:

> During September 16–17, 1876, on the eve of the edifice's dedication, a hurricane blew through the area. Pamlico Sound engulfed Swan Quarter, sweeping the sanctuary off its foundation. A Providence United brochure tells what happened:
>
> "A miracle was happening—the church was floating

down the road. The church 'moved by the hand of God.' It went straight down the road to a corner and bumped into a general store owned by George V. Credle. The corner is now Oyster Creek Road and U.S. 264 Business.

"Then a curious thing happened! The building took a sharp right turn and headed down the road for about two blocks until it reached the corner of what is now Church Street. Then it moved slightly off its straight-line course, took another turn to the left, crossed the Carawan Canal directly in front of the place where people desired the church to be, and settled exactly in the center of the Sam Sadler property, the site which had been refused."[2]

Before it settled, it is said to have miraculously rotated around to face the street and there [it] would stay.[3]

Most likely you've already guessed the outcome: Mr. Sadler changed his mind and sold them the property—exactly what the church founders felt God promised them at the start. Though there is no account of the prayers they prayed, I can imagine them saying, "Now, Lord, You moved on our hearts that You wanted the church on that prime property downtown. We believe You can work a miracle to make it happen." What exuberant shouts of praise must have gone up to heaven when they found out what God had done!

If God did something so supernatural to get Abraham's seed to their "land of promise" and these nineteenth-century saints to their "land of promise," will He not move for you as well? Galatians 3:29 reveals your connection to these ancient stories: "If you are Christ's, then you are Abraham's seed, and heirs according to the promise."

Promises from God are part of the legacy that has passed down to you—from Abraham, Isaac, Jacob, the twelve tribes of Israel, the apostles and early disciples, and all who have been in covenant with God in the past. Living a life of hope, joy, praise, divine intervention, and supernatural manifestation was normal for many of them; now it should be normal for you.

You might say, "It's a way of carrying on the family tradition."

CHAPTER 4

NOT ONE WORD WILL FAIL

O NE OF THE most powerful promise scriptures comes from King Solomon. During the dedication of the temple he worshipfully boasted,

There has not failed one word of all His good promise.

—1 KINGS 8:56, MKJV

I love this passage of Scripture. Originally the king of Israel was referring to just those promises about Israel obtaining the Promised Land. However, Solomon's statement can easily be extended to mean the entire Word of God. Not one word ever has failed. Not one word ever will fail.

Notice the phrase "His good promise" is in the singular. Just as the Bible is the Word of God made up of many words, it is the promise of God made up of many promises—all inspired, all dependable, all trustworthy.

Of course, at this point, most of us could stall, take a deep breath, and say, "What about this…or what about that?" as we bring up some situation when God's promises did not seem to work. Are there other contributing factors we need to consider? Yes, there are. To ensure greater success in seizing what is rightfully ours, we must make up our minds to do the following seven things.

1. Set our priorities in order. (Be submitted.)

"Seek first the kingdom of God and His righteousness, and all these things shall be given to you" (Matt. 6:33).

2. Never give up. (Be tenacious.)

"You need perseverance so that, after you have done the will of God, you may receive the promise" (Heb. 10:36, TLV).

3. Confess God's Word often. (Be consistent.)

"Let us firmly hold the profession of our faith without wavering, for He who promised is faithful" (Heb. 10:23).

4. Thank God in advance. (Be positive.)

"Be anxious for nothing, but in everything by prayer and supplication, with thanksgiving, let your requests be made known to God" (Phil. 4:6, NKJV).

5. Acknowledge divine timing. (Be sensitive.)

We may need to pass through successive stages of life to mature us on our way to a promised goal. God prepares a place for us, but He also prepares us for that place—that the two might coincide perfectly. David is a prime example. He passed through the stages of being a faithful shepherd boy, an overlooked son, a despised brother, a servant to a king, a giant-killer, a persecuted outcast, a mentor of rejects, and, through it all, a worshipper of God before he arrived at the goal of becoming king of Judah and finally king over all of Israel. Reflecting on this truth, he admitted to God, "My times are in Your hand" (Ps. 31:15).

6. Fulfill the conditions. (Be diligent.)

Promises in the Bible are almost always attached to conditions. For the promises to be fulfilled, the conditions must first be met. Here are a few examples from the beatitudes:

+ "Blessed are those who mourn, for they shall be comforted" (Matt. 5:4).

+ "Blessed are the merciful, for they shall obtain mercy" (Matt 5:7).

+ "Blessed are the pure in heart, for they shall see God" (Matt. 5:8).

So to receive the comfort of the Holy Spirit, we must fulfill the condition—mourning over our sins and shortcomings in true repentance and godly sorrow. To obtain His mercy and forgiveness, we must fulfill the condition—being merciful to others (compassionate and willing to forgive). To see God (moving in our lives now and in all His glory at the end of this journey), we must fulfill the condition—possessing a pure heart.

7. Understand the concept of *overlap*. (Be wise.)

Sometimes one promise overlaps another and becomes the dominant promise. For instance, someone might claim the divine pledge "By His stripes we are healed" for a loved one, but instead of a miracle happening, that person passes away (Isa. 53:5). God's promise of healing did not fail. It was overlapped by another promise that emerged superior and dominant—such as 2 Corinthians 5:8: "To be absent from the body" is "to be present with the Lord"—which is an even greater victory.

CHAPTER 5

RECEIVING A NEW IDENTITY

I BARELY MADE IT through my teenage years. Playing keyboard in a rock band in Central Florida earned me the status of a card-carrying member of the flower child generation. Unfortunately it also pushed me to the edge of a dangerous precipice—a near-death experience (NDE) at the age of nineteen. That's when I realized the futility of my life, the emptiness of my goals, and the self-ishness of my heart. I began questioning all my choices and values (more correctly, my lack of values). Though I didn't recognize it at the time, the remorse I began to feel came from God as a gift. Right before going to the cross, Jesus made the following pledge.

> I tell you the truth. It is to your advantage that I go away; for if I do not go away, the Helper will not come to you; but if I depart, I will send Him to you. And when He has come, He will convict the world of sin, and of righteousness, and of judgment.
>
> —JOHN 16:7–8, NKJV

The word *convict* means to convince or persuade someone of guiltiness. Jesus said the helper (the Holy Spirit) would "convict the world of sin"—not just those who are saved. When He ascended to heaven, the "dam" burst and spiritual, living water flooded this planet, wooing and drawing the hearts of men by convincing them inwardly of the awfulness of sin and of their need for righteousness. Many have resisted, but once the "Spirit of promise" was released into the world, the scales dipped dramatically toward the redemption of a fallen race (Eph. 1:13, NKJV).

After my NDE I began feeling completely repulsed by the bad choices I had made in life. However, I really can't take any credit for my change of heart because it wasn't me. It was the promise giver fulfilling Romans 2:4: "The goodness of God leads you to repentance."

Instead of continuing to cater toward my lower nature, I began disciplining my life. I became a passionate seeker of truth. Unfortunately, even though my goal was right, the path I chose was wrong. I met an Indian guru who came to America to spread his ideas about yoga and meditation. That encounter launched me into a full-blown commitment to Eastern religions and New Age spirituality. Eventually I began teaching yoga at four universities and started a yoga ashram (a commune where devotees live and study more intensely) in Tampa, Florida.

Every day from morning till night I was totally focused on attaining a conscious awareness of oneness with God. I used wrong methods (such as chanting mantras), I had wrong ideas, and I read a lot of misleading religious books, but I was desperately searching. That's when another promise began hovering over me.

> You will seek the LORD your God, and you will find
> Him if you seek Him with all your heart and with all
> your soul.
>
> —DEUTERONOMY 4:29, NKJV

Key events started taking place that were far more than coincidences. The *Tampa Tribune* did a half-page article on me. I thought it would dramatically increase my yoga classes. Instead, it alerted the House of Hope prayer group to put me on its twenty-four-hour prayer chain list. After weeks of "soaking" me with intercession, another puzzle piece fell into place.

Out of the blue an old friend wrote me a letter telling me how he had been born again. After several days it dawned on me that maybe, just maybe, I had misinterpreted the message of Jesus. I dedicated an entire day to Him, praying over and over, "If you're really the Savior of the world and the only way to heaven, give me a sign today." That ushered another promise right up to my doorstep.

> Ask and it will be given to you; seek and you will find;
> knock and it will be opened to you.
>
> —MATTHEW 7:7

That afternoon I was hitchhiking to the University of South Florida. (Having renounced all material possessions, I had to walk or hitchhike everywhere.) One of the members of the prayer group (who just "happened" to be a former yoga student) was two miles away, about to walk into a laundromat. God spoke to his heart to instead get back in his van and start driving.

At first Kent questioned what he had heard, thinking it to be completely illogical. Thankfully he finally submitted to that God-sent inspiration. He had no idea what God wanted him to do—until he saw me on the side of the road. Unaware that I was the yoga teacher he'd been praying for, he pulled over and offered me a ride. Stepping up into his van, I saw a picture of Jesus taped to the ceiling and immediately knew it was my answer. Within a few minutes, we were talking about the gospel. That's when he started sharing biblical promises with me, such as the following.

And whoever calls on the name of the Lord shall be saved.
—Acts 2:21

That if you confess with your mouth Jesus is Lord, and believe in your heart that God has raised Him from the dead, you will be saved.
—Romans 10:9

Therefore repent and be converted, that your sins may be wiped away, that times of refreshing may come from the presence of the Lord.
—Acts 3:19

But as many as received Him, to them He gave the right to become children of God, to those who believe in His name: who were born, not of blood, nor of the will of the flesh, nor of the will of man, but of God.
—John 1:12–13, nkjv

That Christ may dwell in your hearts through faith.
—Ephesians 3:17

He who believes in the Son has eternal life.

—JOHN 3:36

As I knelt on the floor of Kent's Volkswagen van, all these promises and many more converged on me like multiple beams from numerous heavenly spotlights all striking one spot. I fulfilled all the conditions. I called on the name of Jesus. I confessed Him as Lord of my life. I believed. I repented. I converted (turning away from sin and turning toward God). I received Him into my heart. I accepted the gift of everlasting life. Then a spectacular change took place as all these promises (as well as many other promises I didn't even know existed) exploded into fulfillment.

My sins were blotted out (wiped out of existence as if they never happened), and a time of refreshing blew into my soul. (I didn't know it then, but the Greek word *anapsuxis*, translated "refreshing," means a recovery of breath—like one who is dead being brought back to life.)

That week I announced my experience of salvation in all my classes and canceled them permanently. I shut down my yoga ashram. I renounced my former beliefs, burning all my books and false images. How could something so radical happen in such a short time? Because of three more promises in the following verse that shined brightly my way.

If anyone is in Christ, *he is a new creation; old things have passed away*; behold, *all things have become new.*
—2 CORINTHIANS 5:17, NKJV, EMPHASIS ADDED

It was not intellectual coercion that caused me to switch religions; it was the supernatural reality of promises coming to pass. (Nineteen have been mentioned so far in this chapter alone.)

I received a new, spiritual identity that day. I was no longer a child of darkness and an heir of the curse that separated man from God. The very moment the everlasting Father brought me into His family, I became one of those highly favored and blessed individuals called the "children of promise" and "heirs of promise" (Gal. 4:28; Heb. 6:17).

These are two of the names that belong to all who have been born again.[1] Promises are very much a part of who we are and what we possess.

Let's explore some of the most powerful, most inspirational promises together so we can receive them by faith and walk in their reality every day. Twenty-five primary promises will be emphasized, but all together we will examine three hundred on this amazing journey through God's Word.

THE PROMISES

. . . by which He has given to us exceedingly great and precious promises, so that through these things you might become partakers of the divine nature and escape the corruption that is in the world through lust.

—2 PETER 1:4

DIVINE REVELATION

*But as it is written, "Eye has not seen, nor ear heard,
nor has it entered into the heart of man the things
which God has prepared for those who love Him." But
God has revealed them to us by His Spirit. For the
Spirit searches all things, yes, the deep things of God.*

—1 Corinthians 2:9–10

I**T IS FITTING** that we begin this section on the promises of God with the passage above. If you are one of God's offspring, He intends to reveal deep things to you. To His original disciples Jesus explained, "It is given to you to know the mysteries of the kingdom of heaven" (Matt. 13:11). Supernatural knowledge is a gift, a "good" and "perfect gift…from above" (James 1:17). When Peter confessed that Jesus is truly the Messiah, the Son of God responded.

> Blessed are you, Simon son of Jonah, for flesh and blood
> has not revealed this to you, but My Father who is in
> heaven. And I tell you that you are Peter, and on this
> rock I will build My church, and the gates of Hades
> shall not prevail against it.
>
> —Matthew 16:17–18

In other words, no one convinced Peter intellectually who Jesus is. That insight came directly from God. This is still the solid rock on which the church is being built.

Those who receive true revelation from God cannot be shaken from their faith. One of the most beautiful verses expressing this idea is Job 32:8: "There is a spirit in man, and the breath of the Almighty gives him understanding."

After Jesus rose from the dead, He visited the Upper Room, where the disciples were waiting. That's when "He breathed on them and said to them, 'Receive the Holy Spirit'" (John 20:22). At that moment, God restored to them what Adam had lost in the beginning. This first man passed deception to us through the fall, but Jesus reversed this curse by breathing the Holy Spirit into His followers to "guide" them "into all truth" (John 16:13; see 1 John 2:27).

Now, every born-again child of God has this inheritance. Yes, the breath of God is within you—inspiring you, enlivening you, opening your heart to embrace the deepest truths that can be experienced in this life. How wonderful is that!

My First Encounter With God-Breathed Revelation

In the very beginning of my walk with God, I had a real struggle over the Bible being the inspired Word of God. Considering it was written by forty authors over a period of around fifteen hundred years, I thought, "How could it be without error? Wasn't it just the opinions of the writers— their personal observations and insights?" It was a mental barrier I just could not get over. Then God granted me a visitation.

In a dream I saw the Lord Jesus standing before me, so radiant with the glory of heaven that it was impossible to make out the features of His face. Suddenly He disappeared, and in His place was an open book with gold lettering I immediately recognized as Hebrew. Most significantly the book was pulsating as if it had a heartbeat, and with every throb a river of light flowed off the pages and into my heart.

I woke up feeling a very intense, supernatural presence pouring into me. I knew it was an undeniable validation that the Bible truly is the Word of the almighty God. Since that experience I have never doubted the divine origin of this holy book.

Now, as we continue this journey together, as we focus our hearts on the most powerful promises in the Bible, let us pray for inspiration (a word that means to breathe into)—and let us expect this internal influence from the Spirit of life.

We are supposed to hear what others cannot hear, see what others cannot see, and receive what only God's chosen can receive.

POWERFUL PROCLAMATION

I proclaim that I have received "the Spirit of wisdom and revelation" from God and that I will know the hope of my calling, the riches of my spiritual inheritance, and the greatness of God's power toward me (Eph. 1:17–19). It has been given to me to comprehend the mysteries of the kingdom of God. Therefore, like Paul, I affirm that "I will come to visions and revelations of the Lord" (2 Cor. 12:1, NKJV). *This is God's promise to me. I claim this supernatural impartation and expect its manifestation in my life.*

Additional Insights: Luke 2:25–32;
1 Corinthians 1:7; 1 Peter 1:13

PROMISE 2

INHERITING GOD'S KINGDOM

*Listen, my beloved brothers. Has God not
chosen the poor of this world to be rich in
faith and heirs of the kingdom which He
has promised to those who love Him?*

—JAMES 2:5

ITHIN OUR FALLEN nature we have no capacity
to believe in the true and living God, so He
first introduces this faith into our hearts as a
"gift" (Eph. 2:8). Those who receive such a generous endow-
ment from the Creator may be impoverished naturally, but
spiritually they become "the rich of the earth" (Ps. 22:29,
NLT). They are far richer than the wealthiest individuals
in this world who do not know God—for all other riches
will eventually fade away, but this supernatural wealth will
endure forever.

Then, in response to the presence of faith in our hearts,
God gives us His kingdom. The word *kingdom* means a
king's domain, which in this natural world includes both
the land mass and the people who live there. Inside the
boundaries of a kingdom the personality of the king domi-
nates everything.

The kingdom of God is a spiritual domain under God's
authority. It is filled with His holy presence and permeated

31

with His personality. For this reason Paul affirmed that "the kingdom of God" is "righteousness and peace and joy in the Holy Spirit" (Rom. 14:17). These are not ordinary human attributes but extraordinary, supernatural expressions of the divine personality: "the righteousness which is from God," "peace of God, which surpasses all understanding," and "joy unspeakable"—all flowing out of "the love of Christ which surpasses knowledge," that we might "be filled with all the fullness of God" (Phil. 3:9, NKJV; Phil. 4:7; 1 Pet. 1:8; Eph. 3:19; see also Mark 12:32–34).

Declaring and establishing the kingdom was the emphasis in Jesus's teaching from the beginning to the end. He came out of the wilderness preaching, "Repent! For the kingdom of heaven is at hand" (Matt. 4:17). The first statement of His first recorded sermon was, "Blessed are the poor in spirit, for theirs is the kingdom of heaven" (Matt. 5:3). Almost every parable began with the statement "The kingdom of heaven is like…" (Matt. 13:31). Finally, after rising from the dead, He spent forty days with His disciples "speaking of the things pertaining to the kingdom of God" (Acts 1:3, NKJV).

The terms "kingdom of God" and "kingdom of heaven" are synonymous, describing the same kingdom by referring to the One who rules over it or the place from which it is ruled. Because it originates in a heavenly realm, whenever it manifests on earth, divine, heavenly influence spills over into earthly affairs. That is why Jesus taught us to pray, "Your kingdom come; Your will be done on earth, as it is in heaven" (Matt. 6:10).

One of the pivotal passages of the New Testament is the conversation Jesus had with a Jewish leader named Nicodemus, to whom He said, "Truly, truly I say to you, unless a man is born again, he cannot see the kingdom of God" (John 3:3).

The Greek word translated "again" is *anothen* and literally means from above. At the precise moment we were born again, we received a new spirit *from above*. We were "delivered…from the power of darkness" and "translated…into the kingdom of his dear Son" (Col. 1:13, KJV; see also John 3:1–7). The word *translated* means to be instantly removed from one state of being to another. Once true lovers of God are "translated" into God's kingdom, they inherit all the glorious things that fill this dimension of existence.

When Jesus sent forth His disciples to preach, saying, "The kingdom of heaven is at hand," He added, "Heal the sick, cleanse the lepers, raise the dead, and cast out demons. Freely you have received, freely give" (Matt. 10:7–8).

In other words, Jesus was saying, "Tell them God can reign as King in their hearts. Tell them they can experience His spiritual kingdom. Tell them all the traits of that kingdom can overflow into their lives. Then show them tangible proof of the practical and powerful ways this kingdom living is evidenced." This is still the will of God for those who are "rich in faith" (James 2:5).

SHARING THE KINGDOM WITH OTHERS

One of my cousins was quite a skeptic when I first approached him with the gospel of the kingdom. Just a few months before, one of his arms developed a strange condition that caused it to wither and draw up to his side. Unable to do his job at the post office properly, he was subsequently laid off. The doctors were baffled. There was no explanation for his ailment. I was scheduled to preach in his area, so I called Chip to invite him to the services. At first he totally dismissed the idea of being healed by God's power, so I was quite surprised when he showed up at church that night, along with his Jewish wife, Kitty, who had never attended a Christian gathering before.

I preached a simple message on the kingdom of God and gave an invitation. Chip rushed to the front, wide-eyed with expectation. When I laid hands on him, he fell out under the power of God and was immediately saved and healed. (His arm returned to normal.) Even though I consider myself a person of faith, I was stunned at how quickly and thoroughly God moved.

Having never witnessed anything like that before, his Jewish wife jumped up to leave. Her eyes happened to glance at the cross on the back wall of the church. From it she heard the audible voice of the Yeshua (Jesus) saying, "I am your Messiah. I love you. Come to Me." Instead of running out, she ran forward and was saved. Soon after that encounter with God she enrolled in Christ for the Nations Institute in Dallas, Texas. Eventually she became a teacher of The Jewish Roots of the Church at a large Charismatic church in Florida.

One breakthrough encounter changed both of their lives dramatically and wonderfully. Jesus first authored faith in their hearts; then He blessed them because of their faith with entrance into His kingdom and an inheritance of its supernatural reality.

> For the kingdom of God is not in word, but in power.
> —1 CORINTHIANS 4:20

POWERFUL PROCLAMATION

I proclaim that God has made me rich in faith. Because of this gift, I have inherited the kingdom of God and everything in it: divine joy, peace, love, knowledge, wisdom, and power. I expect manifestations of the kingdom such as deliverance and healing. My daily affirmation before the King of kings is, "Your kingdom come; Your will be done on earth, as it is in heaven" (Matt. 6:10). Anything contrary to the kingdom must depart from my life in Jesus's name. *This is God's promise to me. I claim this supernatural impartation and expect its manifestation in my life.*

Additional Insights: Isaiah 9:6–7;
Matthew 13:1–23; Luke 11:14–20; Revelation 11:15

SHARING GOD'S THRONE

To him who overcomes will I grant to sit with
Me on My throne, as I also overcame and
sat down with My Father on His throne.

—REVELATION 3:21

W HAT AN AWE-INSPIRING invitation from the Son of God! In the original context the Messiah is encouraging the Laodicean believers that if they overcome a state of spiritual lukewarmness, they will be enthroned with Him in a heavenly sphere. However, this promise was not intended for just one local church in Asia Minor; it belongs to the entire body of Christ.

The very moment we surrendered to our heavenly Father, He "made us alive together with Christ" and then He "raised us up and seated us together in the heavenly places in Christ Jesus" (Eph. 2:5–6). Before that we were separated from God, dominated by sin, controlled by satanic powers, corrupted by the fallen nature, and overshadowed by death. All these things reigned over us from the time we were conceived in the womb. (No wonder we came into this world crying.) Then we discovered God's generous pledge.

He raises up the poor out of the dust and lifts up the oppressed from the dunghill to make them sit with princes and inherit a throne of glory.

—1 Samuel 2:8

The word *poor* is not just talking about those who suffer material lack; most likely it is a reference to those who are "poor in spirit" (those who humbly admit they are helpless and hopeless without God). When we exhibit this attitude, the Almighty promises to lift us from the "dust" of mortality and the "dunghill" of carnality to share His glorious throne. Occupying this spiritual position is not just futuristic. Right here in this present world we can experience all that the throne of God represents.

+ **Divine rest:** calmness of heart, peace that passes understanding, an assurance that God's plan will ultimately prevail

+ **Divine authority:** From the throne of a king decrees are made. Hebrews 1:3 states that Jesus "upholds all things by the word of His power." We who are enthroned with Him also speak with authority and dominion. Our prayer lives should not always consist of pleading with God for help. Under the inspiration and authorization of His Spirit, He encourages us to also decree in His name deliverance, healing, prosperity, and victory.

+ **Divine power:** Believers are endued with power to bring change to the culture around us and to dominate spirits of darkness. When Jesus sent

out His disciples, He "gave them power and
authority over all demons and to cure diseases"
(Luke 9:1). This is still His promise today. He
has commanded His own to "be strong in the
Lord and in the power of His might" and promised, in the last days especially, that "the people
who know their God shall be strong, and carry
out great exploits" (Eph. 6:10; Dan. 11:32, NKJV).
He imparts His power to us. He never would
have declared such a possibility if he did not
intend to follow it up with a performance.

+ **Divine victory:** Because Jesus reigns, we reign—
over sin, over the curse, over satanic plots, over
the weakness of our own flesh, over the failures
of our past, and ultimately over death, hell, and
the grave. Yes, our enemies have truly been made
our "footstool" (Mark 12:36, NKJV).

Acknowledging this "throne position" causes an overflow into every area of who we are—body, soul, and spirit.
Most of the time, the results are invisible and internal—
overcoming ordinary negatives such as depression, self-
condemnation, and fear. At other times, this authority
manifests in visible and evident ways, such as conquering
sicknesses or receiving material breakthroughs. Then there
can be remarkable manifestations of this "throne authority,"
such as what happened during a quite unnerving experience I had shortly after I was saved.

FENDING OFF A DEATH THREAT

I was living at a Christian commune in Oviedo, Florida, but had decided to join the Monastery of the Holy Spirit in Conyers, Georgia. (At the time, I did not understand the differences between Protestant and Catholic doctrine—I just wanted to get closer to God and thought that would be the best way to do it.) A man picked me up hitchhiking and asked, "Where are you going?"

I responded, "Just east of Atlanta, Georgia."

He said, "You're in luck; I'm going all the way there. You won't have to get another ride."

I sank back in my seat and whispered a premature hallelujah.

He told me that first he had to pick up his check from a large construction firm at a site close to where he had been working. After arriving, he walked in a trailer and came out a few moments later, saying, "The check will be ready in about twenty minutes. Let me show you around the site." Everything seemed normal at first. Then abruptly he pulled through an open gate into a large field that had once been cultivated. Bouncing wildly on the old furrows, the whole car was shaking and rattling as we sped forward, driving to the center of the field, where there was a cluster of trees and large bushes.

I was feeling very uneasy and suspicious at that point, but we were going too fast for me to do anything about it. Then, with no warning, he slammed on the brakes and pulled out a switchblade. Peering at me with crazed eyes, he informed me matter-of-factly what his intentions were—to rob me, then kill me.

I had two choices: try to avoid the knife, jump out of the car, and run (but it was a large field, and I knew he could run me down with his car), or take authority in the Spirit. Thankfully one of my early teachers taught me that if I ever had a confrontation with a demon, either directly or in another person, I could completely dominate it through bold proclamation of the Word of God. I had never preached before, but having raised my voice in intercession many times, I felt it would work about the same. I launched into an on-fire message as if I were preaching to a crowd of five hundred people.

> One day you're going to stand before God and give an account for every deed you've done in your body. If you're rejected by God, you'll hear Him say, "Depart from Me, you worker of iniquity; I know you not." Then the angels will cast you into hell, into a fire that will never be quenched. You're possessed with demons, and you need deliverance. You've opened the door to evil, and the only thing that can shut that door is calling on the name of Jesus and being washed in His precious blood.

I kept on in that vein for a few minutes until, much to my surprise, his eyes started watering, and he burst out in tears, saying, "You sound just like my momma." I could hardly believe it. He handed me the knife, then turned around, knelt down on the floorboard, and started sobbing in repentance. For a few seconds I just sat there, stunned—then I rolled the window down and threw the knife as far away as I could throw it. I laid hands on him and began casting out devils and claiming God's intervention. We must have prayed twenty minutes, until he felt assured that God had forgiven him.

Through that pivotal experience I learned at the beginning of my walk how to assert my throne-room authority in God. I never attempted to usurp God's position of absolute sovereignty. God forbid! But I dared to vocally assume the authority He delights to share with His faith-filled offspring. It worked in a very critical moment for me. It can work for you too. You may be surprised at the results.

POWERFUL PROCLAMATION

I proclaim that I am enthroned with the Lord Jesus Christ. I have been spiritually resurrected from the grip of sin and death, and now I am seated in heavenly places where I experience divine rest, divine authority, divine power, and divine victory. Sharing this position of dominion and supremacy with the firstborn Son of God, I claim and decree the Word of the Lord over every area of need. I expect to see miracles of overcoming grace, deliverance, and divine provision. *This is God's promise to me. I claim this supernatural impartation and expect its manifestation in my life.*

Additional Insights: Psalm 29:10;
Jeremiah 17:12; Hebrews 8:1–2; Revelation 20:4

THE HUNDREDFOLD RETURN

So Jesus answered and said, "Assuredly, I say to
you, there is no one who has left house or brothers or
sisters or father or mother or wife or children or lands,
for My sake and the gospel's, who shall not receive
a hundredfold now in this time—houses and brothers
and sisters and mothers and children and lands, with
persecutions—and in the age to come, eternal life."
—**MARK 10:29–30,** NKJV

ANY TIMES I have heard ministers reference Jesus's promise of a hundredfold return to encourage believers to give generously in an offering (not criticizing—I've done it too). Usually the expected result is some astounding financial breakthrough or material increase. However, when I studied the original text, I discovered an interpretation with a surprisingly different emphasis.

Jesus never even mentioned money, and He was not suggesting an exact multiplication of the items He listed—that if you give up one house, you will eventually own a hundred more. He was proposing something altogether opposite—urging His disciples to sacrifice their lives for the kingdom of God. This passage was never intended as a strategy for achieving a greater level of prosperity. (Ask the rich young ruler who walked away that day.)

It was a call to radical discipleship.

What are the benefits Jesus talked about? Primarily He promised that those who make personal sacrifices to promote the gospel will be enriched by the new, godly relationships that result. People who receive their help will open the doors of their hearts and homes. There will be a *hundredfold increase* of fatherly, motherly, brotherly, and sisterly affection as the family of God is enlarged and valuable, long-term, covenant relationships are formed. Those who advance God's kingdom will also be rewarded eternally for their efforts.

Jesus was not implying that His disciples should neglect or abandon their own families—but He was admonishing them to put the work of God first. I fully understand this. Though my wife and children often accompany me in my travels, many times I have driven off from the house or boarded a plane—to speak at some conference, revival, or mission crusade—with a heavy heart because for a few days, or a week or two, we would be apart. (I'm sure their hearts were heavy as well.)

My father was a commander in the Navy, and he often took nine-month tours to the Mediterranean on the naval destroyers he commanded. That was tough on my mother, my three siblings, and me. Still, if he could sacrifice time with his family to the degree he did for the security of a nation that will eventually cease to exist, how much more should I and my family be willing to make sacrifices for a kingdom that will endure forever!

MY MIND-SET FROM THE BEGINNING

Sacrificing for the kingdom of God has been my mind-set and my joy from the beginning. I was saved in the fall of 1970, during the Jesus movement era. Shortly after, I moved to a Christian commune in Central Florida. Most of its nine members worked demanding construction jobs during the day. We gave 90 percent of our paychecks to the work of the Lord, and we had church seven nights a week. We were already extreme in our faith walk, but one night sitting around a campfire, Bob, the commune leader, showed me a statement Jesus made that stirred both of our hearts: "So likewise, any of you who does not forsake all that he has cannot be My disciple" (Luke 14:33).

Bob said, "Do you know anyone doing this?"

I said, "No."

He said, "Let's do it."

I said, "Sure, I'm willing."

It was that simple—a decision made in about two minutes. That week we both gave away all our money to the poor and everything we owned to the needy (including expensive music equipment and a car). All we allowed ourselves was one extra set of clothes and a Bible in a small sack.

We had an invitation to minister at a church in Bloomington, Indiana—almost a thousand miles away. We stepped out on the road, hitchhiking that direction. I still remember the little cardboard sign we held up that said, "Going for Jesus!" We had no idea when we would get to eat or where we would sleep. On our way we preached on street corners and college campuses. It was a holy adventure.

When we arrived in Bloomington, the pastor sent word that he had changed his mind and canceled the revival. That was very discouraging—but I soon learned a valuable lesson: that with Jesus, setbacks become setups. As we walked down the street, near the university, Bob slapped me on the shoulder and said, "Mike, we came to Indiana to preach, so we're going to preach!"

About that time we passed Peoples Park, a grassy corner lot that had been purchased by the yippies (a word for hippies who became politically motivated, usually leaning toward Communism or socialism). There was a big sign in the middle of the lot declaring it was for the free use of the people. Bob looked at me and said, "That's our church." It didn't have carpet, but it was covered with lush green grass. It didn't have a high cathedral ceiling, but it did have a star-studded universal dome overhead. How fitting! In Jericho style we marched around the field seven times, praying in the Spirit and claiming the property for the kingdom. (I have always marveled that God used Communists to provide our first "church.")

After pondering the situation, Bob commented, "Mike, we can't have revival without advertisement." Since we only had fifty cents, I wondered what he planned on doing. Looking inspired, he walked across the street to a dollar store and bought two red markers. Then we walked around a pizza parlor to the dumpster in back, and Bob explained his plan. We pulled out four old pizza boxes (to make signs to prop at each corner of the park) and about forty cardboard beer boxes (for people to sit on). Then we wrote on the pizza boxes.

REVIVAL!
OLD-FASHIONED STREET PREACHING
Miracles, Signs, and Wonders
Healing the Sick
Casting Out Devils
Prophesying
Raising the Dead
Every Night at 7:30

Remarkably about seventy people showed up, all of them hippies, druggies, and flower children into alternate spiritual paths. Most of them lived together in a hippie commune nearby, a large mansion near the university. On the opening night I preached on Jesus's challenge in Mark 8:35: "Whoever would save his life will lose it. But whoever would lose his life for My sake and the gospel's will save it."

After forty-five minutes I gave an invitation, and almost everyone gave his or her heart to the Lord, including a musician who played with a band that opened for Led Zeppelin. Most of the members of the commune were saved, so they invited us to move our ministry location to the mansion. We preached there for a week in outrageous surroundings. That was the beginning of my ministry.

About a month later I was invited to travel around the country with an evangelistic group and began sharing my testimony every week in front of hundreds—sometimes thousands—of people as well as ministering almost daily on the streets. Since then I have preached the gospel throughout most of the United States and in twelve other nations.

I left the predictable life of a construction worker and the comforts of a pleasant and peaceful home in Oviedo, Florida, with nothing but a "hundredfold" promise. It came to pass. Hundreds of people have opened the doors of their hearts and homes and churches to me around the globe. I have thousands of friends in the body of Christ worldwide. So far over seventy thousand people—who, in a sense, are my spiritual children—have found the Lord through my efforts, which is the greatest increase of all.

As Jim Elliot, missionary to Ecuador, so famously pointed out: "He is no fool who gives what he cannot keep to gain that which he cannot lose."[1] That's the hundredfold promise: losing your life to find it.

It can happen in great ways or small. Listen closely to His leading. He may call you to become a radical disciple as well.

POWERFUL PROCLAMATION

I proclaim that I accept the call to the demands of true discipleship. I believe God will grant me a hundredfold return for all the sacrifices I make for His kingdom. I praise Him for the multiplication of blessed, covenant relationships developing through my lifetime that will enrich my journey through this world. I expect to win others to salvation and for doors of opportunity to open before me. Most importantly I believe I will bear fruit that will last eternally. *This is God's promise to me. I claim this supernatural impartation and expect its manifestation in my life.*

Additional Insights: Matthew 19:16–30;
Mark 10:17–31; Luke 14:25–33; 18:18–30

DIVINELY ORDERED STEPS

The steps of a good man are ordered by the Lord.
—PSALM 37:23, NKJV

W EARING A SLY grin, a friend once asked, "Do you know what the ninth beatitude is?" With a skeptical tone, I responded that I did not. He blurted out, "Blessed are the flexible, for they shall not get bent out of shape." We both laughed. Later, though, as I pondered that statement seriously, I realized it contained a kernel of important truth.

Very few believers *are* flexible. Schedules and plans are almost chiseled into stone, with very little, if any, room for the spontaneity of the Holy Spirit. In some ways (as in job commitments) that kind of structure is unavoidable, but in other ways we need to be more pliable, more openhearted, more spur-of-the-moment. Jesus revealed this when He was explaining to a Jewish leader named Nicodemus the effects of spiritual rebirth.

> The wind blows where it wishes, and you hear its sound, but you do not know where it comes from or where it goes. So it is with everyone who is born of the Spirit.
> —JOHN 3:8

The Messiah was proposing that those who are *born of* the Spirit should also be *borne by* the Spirit (carried through life by the strong wind of His purpose). However, for this promise to come to pass, three more conditions, revealed in Proverbs 3:5–6, must also be fulfilled:

> Trust in the LORD with all your heart, and lean not on your own understanding; in all your ways acknowledge Him, and He will direct your paths.

AN UNFORGETTABLE NIGHT IN BOMBAY

I have experienced the reality of all these related promises many times, but one event sticks out in my mind. I was returning to the United States after a monthlong mission trip in India and unfortunately facing a twelve-hour layover at the international airport in Bombay (now called Mumbai). Thankfully the airline on which I was flying had a policy of placing those with a layover of eight or more hours in a local five-star hotel free gratis. Though I felt frustrated by the delay, I would soon discover that it was of God. Unknown to me, the wind of heaven was blowing, and God was ordering my steps.

When we got off the shuttle, my attention was drawn to the upscale restaurant inside the hotel. I quickly noticed the sign announcing that the special that night was steak and lobster. Having been confined to a much simpler diet for weeks (a lot of white rice with beans), I was ecstatic. However, as I walked through the door of the restaurant, I heard a familiar voice changing my decision. My heavenly Shepherd said, "Don't go in there. Go out on the street. I have a work for you to do." I was disappointed. At the time, I really didn't want God altering my path. However, my *disappointment* was about to become a divine *appointment*.

Having no interpreter with me, I assumed that mingling with people outside the hotel would be very challenging, but I knew God had that under control. I sensed demonic strongholds all around me, so I began binding all opposing spirits and confessing to God, "Your kingdom come, and Your will be done on this street, Lord." Over and over I claimed the supernatural manifestation of God's kingdom in an area I felt was relatively void of Christian influence. Then it happened!

A short waiter (about four feet, ten inches) frantically ran up to me out of another high-class restaurant adjacent to the hotel. Startling me with an excited, high-pitched voice, he inquired, "By any chance, are you a Christian?"

Stunned that he would ask such a blunt question, I said, "Yes, I *am* a Christian."

Then he got more specific: "By any chance, are you a Pentecostal preacher?"

Raising my voice higher and louder, I responded, "Yes, I *am* a Pentecostal preacher!"

He immediately voiced his surprising request: "Good, there's a man who needs to get saved right now. Come quickly! Come quickly!"

It was surreal—I could hardly believe what was happening. The man who "needed to be saved" was the owner of the restaurant. The waiter, a Pentecostal believer, had been sharing the gospel with him for two years. When the owner came in that night, he told his waiter, "On my way to work I decided that what you've got is real, and I want it." Intimidated at the thought of praying for his boss, the waiter ran out of the restaurant, hoping there would be someone out there to help him pray.

And I just happened to be walking by, halfway around the world from home.

The owner invited me to sit with him at a concrete table in the alley behind his restaurant. We talked about an hour. Finally he leaned forward with a serious look on his face and said, "I'm ready." We bowed our heads, and he repeated a prayer of faith, receiving Jesus into his heart. He was profoundly touched, changed by the power of God. I could tell that God had moved on him. We worshipped together for five or ten minutes, and then he stood up abruptly and said, "Let's go back to my restaurant."

On our way he whispered, "When we get back, I'm going to close the shutters, lock the door, and turn the lights down real low." I looked at him apprehensively, wondering what he had in mind.

"What happens then?" I questioned.

"Then I'm going to call all my cooks and waiters out, and I want you to tell them what you just told me."

When we arrived, I asked, "What religions are represented in your kitchen?"

"I have several Hindus, a Muslim, a Jain, a Buddhist, and a Catholic," he informed me, as about seven weary workers came into the eating area.

For about an hour I shared the gospel in English, and the newly saved restaurant owner functioned as my translator. Finally I gave an invitation, and every cook and waiter in that swanky restaurant raised his or her hand to receive Jesus. After praying about a half hour, knowing it was my only opportunity, I decided to teach another hour on the baptism of the Holy Spirit. Almost all of them were endued with the power of the Holy Spirit, speaking in tongues. It was around midnight when we finally brought it to a close.

Riding the minibus back to the airport early the next morning, I gazed at the first streaks of sunlight driving the darkness of night away and thought, "What a way to leave the country!" I never missed the high-class dinner. God's plan was a much better feast—a divinely ordered night forever engraved on my heart.

POWERFUL PROCLAMATION

I proclaim that the almighty God is ordering my steps. Because I have been born again, gusts of heavenly wind are constantly blowing through my life, moving me in the direction of the purpose of God. Because I trust the heavenly Father with all my heart and refuse to lean on my own understanding, God is directing my path into supernatural happenings—both big and small—that will establish His kingdom in this world. *This is God's promise to me. I claim this supernatural impartation and expect its manifestation in my life.*

Additional Insights: Romans 8:14; 12:1–2;
Ephesians 2:10; 2 Thessalonians 3:5

THE POWER OF
THE SPOKEN WORD

Death and life are in the power of the tongue,
and those who love it will eat its fruit.

—PROVERBS 18:21

I N THIS VERSE God reveals an exciting and enlightening concept. Words are invisible containers of power—spiritual power—that can manifest in both negative and positive, destructive and constructive ways.

Words can have a death-dealing effect, leading people into darkness, damaging them emotionally, mentally, and even physically. Words can also have a life-imparting effect, resulting in salvation, deliverance, healing, success, prosperity, joy, victory, and an eternal inheritance.

The acronym I often use is WYSIWYG. (Go ahead, try pronouncing that!) It stands for "What you say is what you get!" It is normally pronounced *wizzy-wig*.

Interestingly the Hebrew word for *power* in our key verse is *yad* (pronounced *yawd*), and it means an open hand. Symbolically whatever comes out of your mouth you can open your hand to receive. If you confess strength, open your hand to receive it. If you confess hopelessness, open your hand to receive it.

To a limited degree this is a functional truth for all human beings, not just those who are saved. Positive people tend to get positive results in life. Negative people tend to get negative results. However, the potential for the positive is greatly magnified when someone is born again because only then are we aligned with the Father (begotten by God's Word and filled with God's Spirit).

You need to be more than just curious or intrigued about this concept. The condition attached to the promise is "those who love it eat its fruit." So evidently you must *love* the idea of utilizing the power of words to experience the full results that are possible.

Two other passages reveal conditions that are hinged to this promise.

- **Submission:** "If you abide in Me, and My words abide in you, you will ask what you desire, and it shall be done for you" (John 15:7, NKJV).

- **Faith:** The Lord said, "If you had faith as a grain of mustard seed, you could say to this mulberry tree, 'Be uprooted and be planted in the sea,' and it would obey you" (Luke 17:6).

When Jesus said His words must first abide in us, He must have meant both the written Word of God (the *Logos*) and the living word (the *rhema*—God's personal communications to us). Both are essential. No person can autonomously control his environment and circumstances in life. We must have God's involvement, and we must be in alignment with His word. The balancing scripture is

Lamentations 3:37: "Who is he who speaks and it comes to pass, unless the Lord has commanded it?"

The flip side is also true—we can thwart God's intention to do wonderful things for us with a negative or unbelieving confession. Furthermore, far too often we beg God to speak to our "mulberry trees" (things that seem immovably rooted in our lives) when God told us to do the speaking.

JUST ONE THOUGHT MADE THE DIFFERENCE

I learned the power of words in a remarkable way. My wife, Elizabeth, had to go through oral surgery. To accomplish his goals, the dentist propped her mouth open for about three or four hours. When she came out of surgery, both jaws had popped out of joint. She was in excruciating pain with a serious case of TMJ for about six months, constantly trying to coax her jaws back into place, suffering horrible headaches by the afternoon almost every day. We prayed many times but with no results. Maybe we weren't passionate enough. Maybe we didn't assert enough authority. Maybe they were pleading prayers instead of confessions of faith—I don't know. All I do know is nothing got any better. But we didn't give up. We kept praying and kept believing.

Then something amazing happened. I was teaching on a Sunday morning in a church in Savannah, Tennessee, on the theme of forgiveness. About halfway through the message, I happened to look at Elizabeth. She was grimacing in pain as she tried to shove her jaws back into place (something she went through all day long). A flash of fiery anger went through my spirit—anger at my wife's being in pain, anger that we for some reason had not been able to secure her healing, anger that we were living beneath our inheritance. Then, like a bowstring snapping to shoot an arrow, the words shot through my mind: "She's got to get her healing today!"

As soon as I made that internal declaration of faith, a happy, incredulous look came on her face. Stunned, she softly patted her jaws. Then, shaking her head, she raised her hands and praised God. I knew what had happened but never stopped preaching. After church Elizabeth came to me and said, "Mike, the most wonderful thing happened to me when you looked at me this morning. My jaws popped into place for the first time in six months."

I responded, "I know, honey! I *thought* a miracle your direction."

Later that night I was dwelling on the wonderful way we finally received our breakthrough, and the idea came to me, "If a declaration of faith could be that powerful when it was just a forceful, intense thought passing through my mind, how much more powerful it is when I actually speak God's promises out loud in a forceful way." Jesus awakened this kind of fighting faith in His disciples when He claimed, "The kingdom of heaven has forcefully advanced, and the strong take it by force" (Matt. 11:12).

We need to manifest that kind of attitude with every "powerful proclamation" in this book. Let's declare them boldly and forcefully, expecting heaven-on-earth results.

POWERFUL PROCLAMATION

I proclaim that death and life are in the power (the open hand) of my tongue. I choose to speak life over myself and my loved ones. I speak joy and peace, healing and deliverance, prosperity, power, and victory over every challenge I am facing. By faith I reach up my hand to receive these things. In the name of Jesus I refuse to live beneath my privileges as a child of God. The Word of God abides in me, and I abide in Him. Therefore I ask what I desire, and it shall be done. *This is God's promise to me. I claim this supernatural impartation and expect its manifestation in my life.*

Additional Insights: Deuteronomy 30:19–20; Matthew 8:5–10; 1 Peter 4:11

BECOMING THE RIGHTEOUSNESS OF GOD

God made Him who knew no sin to be sin for us, that we might become the righteousness of God in Him.

—2 CORINTHIANS 5:21

O NE OF THE most amazing provisions of the new covenant concerns believers receiving a status of righteousness in the sight of heaven. Any human being attempting to reach such a lofty goal is traveling on a street named Impossible—for the Bible insists "all our righteousness is as filthy rags" and "there is none righteous, no, not one" (Isa. 64:6; Rom. 3:10; see also Luke 18:27).

After the fall the nature of man, infected with the disease of sin, was in a hopeless condition—corrupted and incurably ill. Then it happened! The Son of God offered Himself as a sacrifice on the cross, absorbing the sin of the entire human race and its resulting judgment, "so that He, by the grace of God, should experience death for everyone" (Heb. 2:9; see also James 1:15).

What happened next was supernatural and miraculous. Our main scripture, 2 Corinthians 5:21, describes the spiritual transfer that resulted: "God made Him who knew no sin to be sin for us, that we might become the righteousness of God in Him."

The righteousness of God? How could that be? That would be the pinnacle of perfection—a righteousness equal to God's own. No human being could ever achieve such a status by self-effort. It would be futile to try. Yet it is freely given to those who believe.

> For if by one man's trespass death reigned through him, then how much more will those who receive abundance of grace and the gift of righteousness reign in life through the One, Jesus Christ.
> —ROMANS 5:17

Yes, in this wonderful era righteousness comes as a gift. When we receive Jesus into our hearts as Lord, we receive a "new spirit" (Ezek. 36:26). This regenerated spirit, also called "the new man," is "created…in true righteousness" (Eph. 4:24, NKJV; see also Titus 3:5). In other words, being newly created, our new nature is infused with the very nature of God.

This results in an inborn desire to walk in righteousness. However, if a saved person fails, this status is not irretrievably lost. Imparted righteousness can always be restored, if a child of God approaches the Father with humility, repentance, sincere love, and faith, "for with the heart one believes unto righteousness" (Rom. 10:10).

THE GRAND EXCHANGE: BEAUTY FOR ASHES

A perfect way of illustrating this "grand and miraculous exchange" happened about six months after Elizabeth and I got married in 1989. We had a small, one-story cinder-block rental home (about nine hundred square feet) that was quite old and literally splitting at the seams. (All four corners had major cracks from the foundation to the roof.) We traveled constantly in evangelism, so it didn't matter to us that much. Besides, Elizabeth is an expert interior design specialist (self-taught), and she made the house look spectacular inside.

Then one week we came home from a ministry trip to the shocking sight of the entire kitchen ceiling having fallen on the floor (apparently because of heavy rains and a leak in the roof). I smiled at my wife and quipped, "Looks like a sign *from above* that we need to find another house." We both forced out some half-hearted laughter, then started picking up the debris.

Evidently one of the next things on our agenda was house hunting. Right at the start God gave me two dreams of the interior of the home we were supposed to acquire. For that reason my spiritual radar was turned on every time we drove around our city. Unfortunately Elizabeth would fall in love with some house for sale or rent and turn to get my reaction, only to see me shaking my head and saying, "It doesn't match the dreams" (which I'm sure was a little frustrating to her). Finally she commented (half jokingly), "Mike, you go find your 'dream house,' and then come and get me. It's not working this way."

Then it happened when we were least expecting it. (Isn't that how God often moves?) One night about nine o'clock we were driving around a nice neighborhood in our city and noticed a house for sale that looked very pleasant on the outside, nestled in a cul-de-sac on a hill with about five big shade trees around it. We walked up and knocked on the door. A gracious soft-spoken young man came to the door and welcomed us in. I looked around his home and immediately knew it was not the layout that matched my preconceived insights. As we turned to leave, he said, "Let me show you a new house, right down the road, that my father and I just built."

I responded, "Oh, no! We could never afford a new house." (Unknowingly I was limiting God.)

He replied, "Well, can I show it to you anyway?" We agreed, drove half a block away, and parked in the driveway of a beautiful gray two-story home. When we walked in the front door, my spirit leaped inside of me. It matched the dreams. The similarity was striking.

Then the young man began telling us the history of the house. His father was a Pentecostal pastor. Everyone who worked on the house was saved and walking with God, and when they laid the foundation, they worshipfully wrote the name of Jesus in the concrete before it hardened and dedicated any family living in the house to the will of God and the blessings of God. I shouted, "Sold! We could spend our whole lives looking for a house with Jesus in the foundation and not find one—and here God led us right to it."

It's a long story, but we ended up buying the house for an incredibly low price, and someone dear to us gave us the down payment—so it all worked out perfectly (something God knew in advance).

So how does that fit in with this chapter? Simple.

For a long time my wife and I put up with inferior living conditions in our old house that had serious problems—until it became unbearable. Then our heavenly Father moved us into a brand-new home that even *smelled* new. Everything was pristine and perfect.

In like manner many of us—to one degree or another—lived in a dilapidated condition spiritually, a cursed state of separation from God that caused life to "fall apart at the seams." We just kept putting up with it until our situations became "unbearable." Then we linked up with God's dream by receiving His divine instructions. He moved us from the old to the new, from corruption to incorruption, from separation to union, from unpleasant surroundings to a pleasant environment, from sin to righteousness. Isaiah 61:3 describes this blessed transition as "beauty for ashes" (giving up the "ashes" of yesterday's defeats for the "beauty" of a life in union with the Creator).

Just like our months of unfruitful house hunting, many of us spent wasted years futilely looking for something better than our broken-down past, but what we found never matched up with God's dream for human beings, and we turned away disappointed. We explored the alternatives—materialism, pleasure, education, philosophy, false highs, and false religions—but none of these things cured our problems, and none could provide a suitable dwelling place in life.

We never could have paid the necessary price for what we needed, but in advance our heavenly Father already worked out the down payment for this great exchange to take place: the cross—where our Savior bore our sins, that He might transfer to us His righteousness.

What a miracle! Now Jesus is in the foundation of our lives, and we live under a canopy of His blessings—simply because we have received that righteousness that comes from God as an inheritance. How wonderful is that!

In the Sermon on the Mount, Jesus said it so powerfully: "Blessed are those who hunger and thirst for righteousness, for they shall be filled" (Matt. 5:6). If you receive an infilling of righteousness, that's not something you do; it's something God does. He is the "filler"; you are the "fillee." You become a vessel filled with the righteousness of God. Once this happens, the everlasting Father expects you, and enables you, to cultivate righteous thoughts, make righteous choices, and live righteous lives—not to earn a status, but as a response of gratitude and worship.

POWERFUL PROCLAMATION

I proclaim that I am "the righteousness of God in Christ." Because I have hungered and thirsted after righteousness, God has filled me with His own righteous nature. Therefore in His sight I am "holy and blameless" (Eph. 1:4). Because of the blood of Jesus flowing through my spirit spiritually, this righteous status is constantly being renewed. For this reason I have constant access into the presence of God and the presence of God can abide in me. I am now His dwelling place. God has created in me the ability and passion to live a righteous life, think righteous thoughts and manifest righteous actions. *This is God's promise to me. I claim this supernatural impartation and expect its manifestation in my life.*

Additional Insights: Genesis 15:1–6;
Matthew 6:33; 1 Corinthians 1:30; Galatians 2:21

CRUSHING SATAN

*And the God of peace will crush
Satan under your feet shortly.*

—ROMANS 16:20, NKJV

IRONICALLY GOD'S FIRST promise of redemption, given after the fall of Adam and Eve, was spoken to the very one who caused the whole fiasco. Even before His prophetic pronouncements to Adam and Eve, the Lord of glory declared to the serpent (the original personification of evil):

> Because you have done this, you are cursed more than all cattle, and more than every beast of the field; on your belly you shall go, and you shall eat dust all the days of your life. And I will put enmity between you and the woman, and between your seed and her Seed; He shall bruise your head, and you shall bruise His heel.
>
> —GENESIS 3:14–15, NKJV

This passage was fulfilled gloriously through the first-born Son of God—that ultimate "Seed of the woman." His heel was "bruised" through the painful penetration of nails on the cross, but simultaneously the serpent's head was "bruised." The good news is Jesus recovered from His bruised heel three days later, but the prince of darkness will never recover from his bruised head. It was fatally crushed when redemptive blood flowed out of the wounds of the Son of God. That very day, the one who previously possessed "the power of death" lost his authority in this realm (Heb. 2:14). Colossians 2:15 explains what the Savior accomplished: "And having disarmed authorities and powers, He made a show of them openly, triumphing over them by the cross."

Even though Jesus stripped satanic powers of their authority almost two millennia ago, strangely the battle continues. The crushing of the enemy's head was not a one-time affair; it is an ongoing process. Collectively the feet of all who are part of the body of Christ are still grinding the serpent's head into the dust until his overthrow is completed at the end of this age. However, we need to remind ourselves often—we are not fighting *for* the victory; we are fighting *from* the victory.

The Scripture states that even before we face future battles, we already "*have* overcome the evil one" because "the word of God lives" in us (1 John 2:14, emphasis added). Whatever satanic wiles we face, there is already a promise in God's Word powerful enough to push us through the deception to sure victory. From heaven's perspective, our victory is sure.

Even though Revelation chapter 12 was written over nineteen hundred years ago, it speaks of the enemy's final defeat in the past tense (as if it has already transpired):

> Then war broke out in heaven…. The great dragon was cast out, that ancient serpent called the Devil and Satan, who deceives the whole world. He was cast down to the earth, and his angels were cast down with him. Then I

heard a loud voice in heaven, saying: "Now the salvation and the power and the kingdom of our God and the authority of His Christ have come, for the accuser of our brothers, who accused them before our God day and night, has been cast down. They overcame him by the blood of the Lamb and by the word of their testimony, and they loved not their lives unto the death."

—REVELATION 12:7, 9–11

These are the three primary weapons that will bring forth the enemy's final and ultimate defeat:

1. The "blood of the Lamb" (which causes us to be "justified"—legally acquitted of all guilt, just as if we never sinned, Rom. 5:9).
2. The "word of [our] testimony" (which is based on the infallible, unconquerable Word of God).
3. The denial of self (living a life devoted to selflessly serving God and serving others, even to the point of death).

When these three elements are fused together, they render a person unconquerable.

MY PERSONAL ENCOUNTER WITH THE DEVIL

I personally learned the power of the blood of the Lamb and the word of my testimony when I had a face-to-face encounter with the prince of darkness. In the middle of the night Satan appeared at the foot of my bed. He didn't have any of the traditional features ascribed to him—shiny red skin; horns; a long, pointed tail; a sharp pitchfork. On the contrary, he appeared somewhat handsome in a rugged kind of way: a dark complexion, a prominent forehead, jet-black straight hair, and a long black cloak. The thing that gave him away was his eyes—so full of hate. Though he spoke no audible words, his eyes were communicating, "I'm going to ruin you. I'm going to destroy you."

I was paralyzed. I couldn't move. The air around my bed was thick with the presence of evil. I couldn't even open my mouth to speak. Then—suddenly—I felt a surge of authority go through my spirit as the Holy Spirit (using the sound of my own voice) spoke the following words: "I conquer you, Satan, through the precious blood of Jesus; it is impossible for you to win."

Until that moment the devil bore an arrogant, fiendish grin. After my rebuke his face contorted into a look of terror. Then a second time, slightly louder, the Holy Spirit spoke the exact same statement through me. "I conquer you, Satan, through the precious blood of Jesus; it is impossible for you to win."

What I saw next stunned me. Satan's eyes, like a burning candle, melted into his cheeks. Then his whole face began melting into his neck. The Holy Spirit surged through me, echoing that declaration a third time (once again, using the sound of my own voice). "I conquer you, Satan, through the precious blood of Jesus; it is impossible for you to win."

After that last and loudest rebuke I watched the prince of darkness melt into the darkness, overthrown by the superior authority that resides in the Word of God and the precious blood of the Lamb of God. That night especially I followed the example of thousands of others through the centuries who have received by faith the following pledge Jesus made to His disciples.

> Look, I give you authority to trample on serpents and scorpions, and over all the power of the enemy. And nothing shall by any means hurt you.
>
> —Luke 10:19

"Serpents and scorpions" are symbolic of evil spirits who are subordinate to that "ancient serpent" (Satan), whose goal is to entice human beings to pursue their lusts and commit evil. Their poisonous venom is sin, "and when sin is finished, it brings forth death" (James 1:15). The consecrated sons and daughters of the new covenant are the serpent-bruisers of this era. We are not afraid of their venom, for we have found the antidote.

Jesus began this act of crushing Satan and his subordinate demons underfoot when He was in the world; now we are continuing the process—until it is completed at the end of this age. All satanic forces are "anti-Christ" spirits, for they fight against the Christ (the Messiah, the anointed One) and His anointed followers. Therefore they must bow before the ancient declaration in 1 John 4:4: "You are of God, little children, and have overcome them, because He who is in you is greater than he who is in the world." (See 1 John 4:1–3.)

I questioned God one time in prayer about that statement in Luke 10:19: "Nothing shall by any means hurt you." I complained, "Something's wrong, Lord, because I've been hurt. I've been damaged by demonic attacks on my life and my walk with You."

His response was powerful. I heard Him speak unmistakably to my spirit, "They may have had power to hurt you temporarily, but they had no power to harm you permanently." After the dust of war has settled at the end of this age, we will certainly be able to shout with bold finality, "*We win!*"

THREE IMPORTANT POINTS

As this chapter comes to a close, we need to revisit our foundation scripture and ponder three more vital truths revealed through it: "And the God of peace will crush Satan under your feet shortly" (Rom. 16:20, NKJV).

+ **The God of peace**—Notice it is not "the God of war" but "the God of peace" who promises to crush Satan. The Creator is not fearful, nervous, anxious, or stressed about the battle nor its outcome. He is calm, assured, and fully confident of His superior authority and the supremacy of His plan. If He can be at peace in the midst of furious satanic assaults, we can be at peace as well.

+ **The God who uses people**—Notice God is the One who is crushing Satan, but He does it under our feet. This passage does *not* say, "The God of peace will crush Satan under *His feet*." It declares that this will happen under "*your feet*." God's delight is for us to participate in the process of reclaiming this world for the kingdom of heaven.

+ **Two important prerequisites**—Carefully read the verse that comes before our primary scripture. The writer pleads, "I want you to be wise to that which is good, and innocent to that which is evil" (Rom. 16:19). Immediately after these words the Satan-crushing promise is given—so they reveal the dual condition of the promise coming to pass.

POWERFUL PROCLAMATION

I proclaim that the God of peace has empowered me for war. This conflict is not against flesh and blood but against powers, principalities, and spiritual wickedness in high places. I make a commitment to be wise concerning good, to be innocent concerning evil, and to live a selfless life. I trust in the blood of Jesus and the Word of God. Therefore by all these things I have superior authority over all satanic forces that plot against me. As far as heaven is concerned, I have already overcome—for greater is He who is within me. *This is God's promise to me. I claim this supernatural impartation and expect its manifestation in my life.*

Additional Insights: Psalm 91:11–13;
Isaiah 27:1–3; Mark 16:17–18; Luke 10:17–20

EXCEEDINGLY
ABUNDANTLY BEYOND

Now to Him who is able to do exceedingly
abundantly beyond all that we ask or imagine,
according to the power that works in us.

—Ephesians 3:20

IN THIS ENCOURAGING verse three strong power words are grouped together in one intense statement: *exceedingly*, *abundantly*, and *beyond*. *Exceedingly* means to an unusual degree. *Abundantly* means generously, lavishly or profusely. *Beyond* means surpassing all limitations.

Ponder those definitions for a moment. Then imagine— imagine what God could do in your life, what answers He could send to your prayers. Now bump it up several notches beyond what you even think is possible. Let your faith rest there—on the exceptional, the extraordinary, the supernatural—realizing this promise is dependent on the "power that works in us." What power? The power of hope. The power of faith. The power of positive confession. The power of tenaciously holding on. The power of thanksgiving and praise. The power of expecting God to be God. These are all small linked gears that move a machine much bigger than themselves.

A MIRACLE IN BARABOO

Let me share with you how this verse was fulfilled for me gloriously, even when I *didn't believe*. Right after I found the Lord, I was consumed with a passion to win my entire family. I became very vocal with my loved ones. All my siblings, cousins, aunts, and uncles heard a clear presentation of the gospel from me, and many of them came to Jesus, but one of my favorite uncles lived way up in Baraboo, Wisconsin (which was a small community in a rural area on the way to a popular attraction called the Wisconsin Dells).

I would pray, "God, I ask You to send just one born-again believer to Uncle Dick to share the gospel with him"; then my voice would trail off because the negative thought would echo in my mind, "There aren't any born-again believers in Baraboo." Faith just did not arise. Finally I decided to take things into my own hands and drive up to Wisconsin from Tennessee. However, unknown to me, my heavenly Father had already orchestrated a miraculous answer. About two weeks before my road trip a bus carrying about twenty believers on their way to a retreat at the Dells broke down just a couple of miles away from my uncle's trailer.

That's not all. My uncle's mechanically inclined son-in-law, who lived next door, just "happened to be" the one who stopped to help the stranded travelers. Though they had no money for repairs, he compassionately pulled their broken-down bus with a chain to his yard and for many days worked on it diligently. Since there was no place for the group to stay, my gracious uncle and his son-in-law and daughter let them all stay in their trailers. With a doubtful heart, I had asked God to send one born-again believer, and He sent almost two dozen Christians—who held daily worship sessions, prayer meetings, and Bible studies and shared the gospel with them all. I arrived shortly after they had all departed (feeling quite useless after I heard what God had done). Wow! I had to repent because I knew I had "limited the Holy One of Israel" (Ps. 78:41, kjv). He's God. He created the entire universe. He can miraculously and abundantly meet your need. Just release the power of faith within.

POWERFUL PROCLAMATION

I proclaim that my God is able to do exceedingly abundantly above anything I could ask or imagine. I refuse to limit God with small thinking. I release the power within—the power of faith activated by praise—fully expecting God to be the Almighty, all-powerful and all-sufficient. Jesus came to bring us a life of abundance, so I receive it by faith. *This is God's promise to me. I claim this supernatural impartation and expect its manifestation in my life.*

Additional Insights: Psalm 36:7–8;
Mark 9:23; John 10:10; 1 Timothy 1:14

PROMISE 10

ANGELIC INTERVENTION

But to which of the angels did He at any time say: "Sit at My right hand, until I make Your enemies Your footstool"? Are they not all ministering spirits sent out to minister to those who will inherit salvation?

—**HEBREWS 1:13–14**

PSALM 33:6 EXPLAINS that all the host of heaven were created with the "breath" of God's mouth (from the Hebrew word *ruach*, also translated *Spirit* and *wind*). Imagine millions of radiant, angelic entities flashing into existence as God "exhales" into the vastness of His universe, resulting in waves of grateful praise cascading upward toward His throne. What a powerful image!

In the Bible angels fill seven primary roles: worshippers, warriors, watchers, messengers, ministers, protectors, and administrators of God's affairs in heaven and in earth. In our main passage above they are identified as "ministering spirits"—because the sole purpose of their existence is to minister to God above and to human beings below. Angels even ministered to the Son of God when He was in the wilderness being "tempted by Satan" (Mark 1:13). We are not told exactly how they helped Him—but the point is this: if He who was perfect benefited from the ministry of angels, we who are so imperfect certainly need their intervention.

The Bible records many instances when angels were sent to assist God's people (like the one who shut the lions' mouths for Daniel, the one who rescued Peter from prison, or the one who rolled the stone away from the tomb where Jesus's body was buried—Dan. 6:22; Acts 12:1–11; Matt. 28:2–4). They are God's "servants who do His pleasure" (Ps. 103:21). You can expect them to assist you too.

> For He shall give His angels charge over you to guard you in all your ways. They shall bear you up in their hands, lest you strike your foot against a stone.
>
> —Psalm 91:11–12

Angels "excel in strength" (Ps. 103:20, NKJV). It only took one to conquer the entire Assyrian army, and it will only take one to bind Satan in a bottomless pit at the close of this age. (See Isaiah 37:36 and Revelation 20:1–3.) No wonder they are called "mighty angels" (2 Thess. 1:7).

Angels are under God's authority alone. There is no record of any human being ever commanding angels to do their bidding, or anyone attempting to communicate with angels unless they start the conversation. Though traditionally they are always depicted with wings, only the highest orders (seraphim and cherubim) are described this way in Scripture (Isa. 6:1–2; Ezek. 1:6; 10:1–8).

When they manifest in this natural world, sometimes they appear as celestial beings—as did Gabriel when he communicated to Mary that she would be the mother of the Son of God. At other times they assume human form—as happened when they visited Abraham and soon afterward rescued Lot and his family from Sodom. (Read Genesis 18:1–19:22.) In the latter circumstance they were even described as both "angels" and "men" (Gen. 19:15–16). No wonder the Scripture admonishes us, "Do not forget to entertain strangers, for thereby some have entertained angels unknowingly" (Heb. 13:2). This tells us they can be mistaken for actual human beings.

THE ANGEL SAID, "YOU'RE NOT ALONE!"

Such was the visitation my wife, Elizabeth, received during one of the most challenging times of her life. During a routine checkup a large tumor was discovered in one of her breasts. The implied prognosis was not good. She might have only a few months. She was shaken. It was October of 2011.

A few days later, after a follow-up appointment, she entered an elevator at Memorial Hospital in Chattanooga. She doesn't remember seeing anyone else being in the elevator when she stepped in. For that reason when the elevator doors closed, she was startled by the words: "Honey, you look like you need a hug."

She turned to see an older woman with gray hair twisted and stacked on her head in a traditional "religious" style (like the women of the country church she attended as a child). She looked very proper, with a long red skirt below the knees, and a white blouse framed with ruffles at the wrists and a high ruffled collar around the neck, adorned by a red shoestring bow.

My wife is not the kind of person who allows strangers

into her "personal space." But in a break from the norm, she responded, "Yes, I do."

The woman came over, hugged her, and said, "You're not alone, and everything's going to be OK."

She felt a calmness come over her. Stepping out of the elevator, she thought, "I need to thank her," and turned around, only to see an empty elevator and empty halls on either side. There was nowhere she could have gone. The lady simply vanished.

Elizabeth is convinced (and I am too) that it was an angel. By the way, at the time of this writing it's been seven years, and my wife is still cancer-free. God was with her, and everything really did turn out OK, just as the angel foretold. What a mysterious way God devised to prophesy this outcome!

POWERFUL PROCLAMATION

I proclaim that because I am an heir of salvation, ministering spirits are active all around me, bringing heaven-sent deliverance and blessings into my life. God has even "charged" His angels to guard me in all my ways, to prevent harmful things from happening to me. Certain angels are assigned to me who minister to me and for me; they always behold the face of the Father in heaven and are ever ready to intervene on my behalf. *This is God's promise to me. I claim this supernatural impartation and expect its manifestation in my life.*

Additional Insights: 1 Kings 19:1–8;
2 Kings 6:8–23; Psalm 34:7; Matthew 18:10;
24:31; 25:31; Revelation 12:7–10

PROMISE 11

BLESSED WITH ALL
SPIRITUAL BLESSINGS

*Blessed be the God and Father of our Lord Jesus
Christ, who has blessed us with every spiritual
blessing in the heavenly places in Christ.*

—EPHESIANS 1:3

THERE ARE THREE aspects to this amazing promise.
First, it is worded in the past tense—the Father
already *has* blessed us. (Technically this is called the
present perfect tense because it describes something that
starts in the past but continues into the present—which is
a perfect description of God's provisions.) Believers who
comprehend this truth no longer plead with God to pour
out these spiritual blessings. Instead, they praise Him for
the manifestation of what they already possess.

Second, He has blessed us with *every* spiritual blessing—
so absolutely nothing has been left out. The entire spectrum
of spiritual realities that bring wholeness and fullness to us
have already been deposited in our heavenly "bank account":
forgiveness, cleansing, love, joy, peace, imparted righteousness, holiness, strength, wisdom, knowledge, soundness of
mind, power, authority, and so much more. All we need to
do is fill out a "withdrawal slip," put our signature on it, and
by faith receive what rightfully belongs to us.

Third, this inheritance is accessed in "heavenly places in Christ." Those who are part of the body of Christ have been given entrance rights into a supernatural realm that the people of this world don't even know exists. This astounding birthright comes to us the moment we are saved, as the following verses indicate.

> But God, being rich in mercy, because of His great love with which He loved us, even when we were dead in sins, made us alive together with Christ (by grace you have been saved), and He raised us up and seated us together in the heavenly places in Christ Jesus.
>
> —Ephesians 2:4–6

When believers sit with one another—talking about the things of God, worshipping together—His love and grace pass between us, and a heavenly atmosphere swirls around us. Angels draw near, the two worlds merge, and God's blessings overflow. Jesus even promised, "Where two or three are assembled in My name, there I am in their midst" (Matt. 18:20).

This is all about identification with the Messiah. Read Ephesians 2:4–6 again carefully. Our God has "made us alive" together with the Messiah.

+ When we identify with Him in His resurrection, we are resurrected from the death-dealing effects of sin.

+ When we identify with Him in His ascension, we ascend in our spirits into heavenly places.

+ When we identify with Him in His enthrone-
  ment (His dominion, authority, rest, and victory over all things), we are enthroned with Him
  on high. In that spiritual position dominion,
  authority, rest, and victory overflow into our
  hearts and lives.

Many students of the Word call this "the ascended
life," laying claim to all the wondrous blessings that are
waiting for us in the celestial realm. Psalm 68:18 prophesied in advance that when the Messiah "ascended on high,"
He would lead "captivity captive." In other words, as He
reassumed His throne, this victorious conqueror of death,
hell, and the grave imprisoned everything that could ever
potentially imprison His people—both before and after
salvation—so that we can enjoy heavenly glory, peace, bliss,
and freedom right here during our pilgrimage on earth—
even during challenging times.

Earthly Fears Calmed by
a Heaven-Sent Visitation

There is no better example of this triune promise coming
to pass than when my wife, Elizabeth, was diagnosed with
cancer in October of 2011 (shared in the previous chapter).
She had already received an angelic visitation, so God-sent
faith was filtering through her doubts and fears, empow-
ering her with a positive mind-set. Then the Lord sent a
second witness of His intention to intervene.

She was about to undergo a scheduled PET scan.
Ironically it was on a Black Friday and was all the more a

dark time for her. As she was being drawn into the internal part of an imaging machine, she distinctly heard orchestral music playing "The Old Rugged Cross."

Surprised, Elizabeth questioned the attendant, "Do you play music in here?"

Slightly annoyed, he responded, "No ma'am, you will have to be still, or we will have to do this all over again."

The music faded out, but then another song filled the room with numerous instruments playing "Here I Am to Worship." Not just surprised but stunned, Elizabeth asked again, "Where is this music coming from?"

Tensely the machine operator replied, "Ma'am, we don't play music in here—you will have to be still."

A peaceful smile came across her face. She knew. It was music from another world. God was speaking to her supernaturally (not just once but twice—for God usually gives two or three witnesses on important matters). It was a double prophecy that if she would *cling to the old rugged cross*, and the price that was paid there, she would be healed—and that the whole affair would ultimately result in *worship* ascending out of her heart.

Yes, it was an *earthly place* of extreme stress and worry, but for a beloved daughter of God, it became a *heavenly place* in Christ, a place of communion with God, a place of promises coming to pass.

POWERFUL PROCLAMATION

I proclaim that I am already blessed with all spiritual blessings in heavenly places in Christ. All the infillings I need—peace, joy, love, strength, wisdom, and much more—already belong to me. Because I identify with the resurrected Savior, I am resurrected in Him. Because I identify with the Lord of lords in His ascension, I rise above all the negatives in my life. Because I identify with Jesus in His enthroned state, I am seated with Him in heavenly places, where I enjoy wholeness and fullness. I choose to maintain this "ascended" mind-set. *This is God's promise to me. I claim this supernatural impartation and expect its manifestation in my life.*

Additional Insights: Psalm 46:1–4;
John 1:16; Hebrews 3:1; 12:22–24

SPIRITUAL REVIVING

*For thus says the High and Lofty One who inhabits
eternity, whose name is Holy: "I dwell in the high
and holy place, with him who has a contrite and
humble spirit, to revive the spirit of the humble,
and to revive the heart of the contrite ones."*

—ISAIAH 57:15, NKJV

THE WORD REVIVAL has been used so much it has lost its intensity of meaning. To be revived literally means to be restored back to life, to be raised from the dead. A true revival is much more than a series of evangelistic meetings believers attend at some local church. A true revival is a spiritual resurrection, an awakening of destiny, purpose, and fervency toward God.

Notice God attaches two conditions to this promise.

+ First, the seeker must approach God with a "contrite spirit." The word *contrite* means an attitude of godly sorrow, being grief-stricken and repentant over sins or shortcomings.

+ Second, the seeker must approach God with "humility." The word *humble* comes from the word *humus*, meaning ground or dirt. The humble person is one who gets down to "dirt level,"

acknowledging his utter dependency on God and
his utter helplessness without the Creator's help.

Those who humble themselves "in the sight of the Lord"
(acknowledging His omniscience) and "under the mighty
hand of God" (acknowledging His omnipotence) have a
promise of being "lifted up" and "exalted" to "the high
and holy place" (the heavenly realm) where God's Spirit
and God's Word "revive" the broken and bruised heart,
restoring it to a state of righteousness in the sight of heaven
(James 4:10; 1 Pet. 5:6; Luke 14:11). The weak are made
strong. The depressed are made joyful. The defeated are
made victorious. Alive again!

FROM ADDICTION TO LIBERATION

I have seen this supernatural reality evidenced over and
over again—including a number of incidents in my own
family. Right after I found the Lord, I began claiming that
promise, "Believe in the Lord Jesus Christ, and you and
your household will be saved" (Acts 16:31). I would often
make the declaration, "I claim my brother, my sisters, every
uncle, aunt, and cousin for the kingdom of God," and then
call them all by name. Many experienced salvation through
my witness, but none was as radical a change as one par-
ticular cousin who had a high-paying corporate position,
a nice home, a wife, and children. Then he began experi-
menting with drugs, first marijuana, then pills, then acid,
then heroin. The hole just kept getting deeper, eventually costing him about $250 a day to satisfy its demands.
It wasn't long before he lost everything and was living on

the street in an old beat-up Volkswagen bug. But he had a cousin claiming his soul for salvation.

One morning he felt strangely compelled to visit an uncle he hadn't seen in about ten years (my father, Andrew Shreve). He drove all day to Orlando, Florida, and arrived at about nine o'clock that night. I just happened to be in Orlando that weekend participating in a series of revival meetings and staying with my parents. (I love it when a coincidence is really a God-incidence.) When I got back home at about eleven o'clock, my cousin was sitting there. I could tell he was high—I found out later he shot up some heroin before he got to the house—so I waited for my parents to go to bed. Then I shared my concerns about his choices in life and what true biblical salvation was all about. After about a half hour he said, "I'm ready, man"—so we went to our knees, and I led him in a prayer of salvation.

I will never forget what happened next. He looked up at me startled and said, "I'm not high anymore, and I feel this power in the air all around me."

I said, "That's the sweet Holy Spirit, and He feels even better when He comes on the inside."

He said, "Let's go for it, man," and started praying like a pro. Suddenly, with astonishment written all over his face, he stopped praying, then, stumbling over his speech, said, "I just had a…I just had a…it was more real than a hallucination…it was like a…like a—"

I interrupted, "Like a vision?"

"Yeah, that's it! I think I just had a vision."

I got excited then and said, "Tell me about it."

What he shared convinced me more than ever that God is a genius at talking to people on their level (like the Son of God conveying eternal truths to fisherman and farmers by sharing parables about their trades). He said, "You won't believe this, but I saw me and the Lord in a wrestling ring. He had me in a half nelson with my shoulders on the canvas, and I was crying, 'Uncle, uncle!'"

I knew that meant, "I give up! I surrender," so I said, "Everyone I know gets saved crying, 'Jesus,' but if you can get saved crying, 'Uncle,' you just go right ahead."

It was all quite amazing. He really did get saved. He quit heroin that night and never went through any withdrawal symptoms. (God still works miracles!) Three weeks later he was baptized in the Holy Spirit, and then he received a calling to preach. He had fallen into a low place of degradation and evil, but he came to God with a humble and a contrite heart. God lifted him to the high and holy place—into His own glorious presence—gave him a "new spirit," and revived his heart, resurrecting him from the death of sin to the life of a righteous standing in the sight of heaven. God removed from him the "stony heart" of rebellion and gave him a "heart of flesh"—a sensitive, feeling heart yielded to the will of God (Ezek. 11:19).

God will revive your heart as well—no matter what you have been through. Just say, "Uncle."

POWERFUL PROCLAMATION

I proclaim that because I have approached God with godly sorrow for the errors of my past and humbled myself under His mighty hand, He has lifted me to the high and holy place, where He daily revives my heart and my spirit. Death was vanquished when my Savior rose from the grave, so now that I am in Him, I am healed of all the death-dealing blows I have received in this world. My faith, love, joy, hopes, and dreams are resurrected to life in Him. *This is God's promise to me. I claim this supernatural impartation and expect its manifestation in my life.*

Additional Insights: Psalm 85:6; 91:1; 143:11; 2 Corinthians 1:8–10; Colossians 2:13–15; 3:3

GOD TURNS CURSES
INTO BLESSINGS

We know that all things work together for
good to those who love God, to those who
are called according to His purpose.

—ROMANS 8:28

READ OUR OPENING verse above slowly, absorbing every word. When God said "all things," He meant it—and that includes the most painful disappointments and hurts you could ever face in life. Our Father is an absolute genius at turning negatives into positives, burdens into bounty, ashes into beauty, darkness into light, and empty space into a magnificent universe that defies description. He certainly proved that in the beginning, didn't He?

Another way of declaring this wonderful truth is found in Deuteronomy 23:5:

Nevertheless, the LORD your God would not listen to Balaam. Instead the LORD your God turned the curse into a blessing on you because the LORD your God loves you.

This intriguing passage refers to Numbers 22–24, chapters that deal with Balaam, the backslidden prophet, trying to call down enchantments on Israel at the king of Moab's request. With each attempt Balaam was thwarted in his witchcraft and instead received a true oracle from God foretelling the ultimate victory that Israel would experience.

Several years ago, as I was preparing a message on this theme, God interrupted my thoughts and said, "I always do that; I always turn every curse into a blessing in the lives of My people." That word from God gripped me, captivated my mind, and compelled me to search God's Word for supportive evidence. I found an abundance.

One of the prime examples is Joseph. Betrayed by his brethren, he was sold into slavery and carried into Egypt (a curse indeed!). Even though he faithfully served Potiphar, the captain of the guard who purchased him, he was falsely accused of making advances toward Potiphar's wife and thrown into prison (another curse indeed!). There he prophesied to Pharaoh's chief butler and chief baker, urging them to remember him to those in authority. Instead, they forgot their commitment to him altogether (a third curse!). Yet God used all these apparent "curses" to weave His will and purpose into the lives of Joseph and his family (even those who cruelly mistreated him). What an amazing God we serve!

Later, after Joseph was brought out of prison to interpret Pharaoh's dreams and was made Pharaoh's subordinate ruler over all the land, his brothers begged to be forgiven, but he responded,

> You intended to harm me, but God intended it for good, in order to bring it about as it is this day, to save many

lives. So now, do not fear. I will provide for you and your
little ones.

—Genesis 50:20–21

And he did. Joseph took care of his parents and all his
brothers and their families during seven years of famine.
The children of Israel prospered and multiplied when they
all should have perished.

Threatened by the American Atheists

After finding multiple witnesses in Scripture, I looked
at my own life and found numerous incidents where this
promise was present—invisible, subliminal, flowing like a
deep, still current when chaotic waves were crashing on the
surface that seemed completely unmanageable.

A good example is the time Madalyn Murray O'Hare,
founder and president of the American Atheists, threat-
ened me with legal action in 1981. As an outreach of my
evangelistic work, for over ten years I conducted drug abuse
assemblies in middle schools and high schools throughout
the United States and overseas. Thousands of students gave
their hearts to the Lord as a result. A team of former drug
users and addicts accompanied me, sharing their testimonies and music. It was very effective. Back in the '70s and
'80s principals were so desperate for help during the drug
epidemic, they would allow us to give invitations for salvation and hold hour-long prayer meetings with the students
after the presentation without any qualms. In some places
nearly the entire student body of a school sought God for
salvation.

Once I spoke in Thomasville, North Carolina, at several schools with very favorable results. In the local high school about three hundred students gave their hearts to the Lord, kneeling on the bleachers in the gymnasium. The local newspaper carried a positive story, applauding our efforts. Everyone seemed to agree it was wonderful—that is, until the superintendent, the principal, and I all received similar letters from Madalyn O'Hare threatening legal action. I still have the original letter, typed on American Atheists letterhead, communicating Mrs. O'Hare's threat.

Mr. Shreve:

It has come to our attention that you…have been entering certain public schools throughout the country with an alleged "drug abuse" program…for the introduction of the mental drug of religion. We have been appalled at what has been reported to us, concerned with your unprincipled and unAmerican activities…a law of the land is being violated.…This cannot be condoned.…We feel the need for restraining legal activities should you continue with these violative procedures. Please send a list of projected appearances so that we may meet you with legal services there.

In response to her request, I put her on our mailing list, and she began receiving a Christian magazine we published bimonthly that contained my revival itinerary (not exactly what she wanted—but certainly what she needed).

Back in Thomasville my story was in the editorial column of the local newspaper several times every week.

In one issue they would publish letters to the editor from those who lambasted me for bringing religion in the schools. The next week they would publish letters from those who were very appreciative that I had made such an exceptional impact.

It went on for about six months—pro and con—before it dawned on me that I needed to capitalize on all this free publicity. I called Madalyn's son, Bill Murray (the very one she took to the Supreme Court when he was a boy in her quest to have prayer thrown out of schools). Ironically later in life he was born again and became actively involved in trying to get prayer back into schools. (God does have a sense of humor, doesn't He?) I asked if he would be interested in speaking for me at an America for Jesus tent rally. He enthusiastically agreed. We ended up having one of the biggest tent meetings that little city in North Carolina has ever seen. I learned the power of believing in Romans 8:28: "We know that all things work together for good to those who love God, to those who are called according to His purpose."

This is the dual conclusion of the matter:

- God turns curses into blessings because He loves us.
- God makes all things work together for our good because we love Him.

In the final analysis both of these promises work because of the power of love.

POWERFUL PROCLAMATION

I proclaim that God loves me with an everlasting love and He will turn every curse that comes my way into a blessing, one way or the other. No weapon formed against me will prosper. No satanic agenda will succeed. All things will work together for my good because I am called for a divine purpose. Every setback is really a setup for divine intervention. Every test will become a testimony of His power. *This is God's promise to me. I claim this supernatural impartation and expect its manifestation in my life.*

Additional Insights: Numbers 22–24;
Romans 8:28–39; 2 Corinthians 4:17

Promise 14

INHABITING OUR PRAISE

*But You are holy, O You who
inhabits the praises of Israel.*

—Psalm 22:3

God promises to dwell in the praises of His
people. When we lift our voices to adore Him,
magnify Him, and glorify His name, He pours
His powerful presence into our words and hearts, so it
spills over into the atmosphere around us. That's what a
real church service is all about, or any time of passionate,
personal prayer.

I especially like the Modern King James translation of
this verse:

But You are holy, enthroned on the praises of Israel.

God promises to seat Himself on the "throne" we build
for Him through worship—reigning as King in our midst
by radiating His dominion, expressing His power, and covering everyone with His peace—when we gather together
in His name. What a powerful combination: our hearts
poured upward and God's heart poured downward! That's
when the two worlds merge. Eternity and time come
together; heaven and earth blend. His kingdom comes, and
His will is done, on earth as it is in heaven.

A Unique, Heaven-Sent Visitation

I saw this demonstrated in an amazing way in People's Cathedral, one of the most prominent Pentecostal churches on the island of Barbados. On a Friday night while I was ministering, the presence of God suddenly gripped the congregation. I couldn't preach anymore. Passionate praise began ascending upward. It went on and on. The worshippers kept lingering with uplifted hands. No one wanted to stop.

Then a very peculiar thing took place. I began hearing the unmistakable sound of a shofar being expertly and loudly played. I peered all over the room, even looking behind some large pillars in the middle of the sanctuary, trying to see who was blowing the traditional Israeli instrument. After a few minutes the only Messianic Jewish person in the room, Roberta Simpson, ran up to me. Excitedly she asked, "Do you hear that shofar?"

I said, "Yes, I do!"

She responded, "Nobody here owns one—and if they did, they wouldn't know how to play it." Both of us grasped the profoundness of what was happening, and our faces reflected the awe we felt. Heaven was invading earth, and we were blessed to be hearing a supernatural instrument, just as they did at Mount Sinai. (In Exodus 19:19—most English versions say a "trumpet" sounded from Mount Sinai on the day God gave the Ten Commandments, but the original Hebrew word is *shofar*.)

Soon after, a lengthy prophetic word flowed out of me. Toward the end of it God said, "Thus says the Lord, set yourself, prepare yourself, for the third day, for I will surely visit you" (again, reminiscent of the timing at Mount Sinai—Exodus 19:10–25). Sunday (the third day) arrived, and we came to church with elevated expectations.

The two morning services were wonderful but nothing extraordinary. We were all slightly disappointed, wondering when the word of the Lord would come to pass. (Sometimes God likes to keep us on the proverbial edge of our seats.) That night we returned for the five o'clock and seven o'clock services. (The church could only hold about one thousand people, and usually about double that attended.) I preached on our calling to be "The Mighty," from the King James Version of Psalm 29:1–2:

> Give unto the Lord, O ye mighty, give unto the Lord glory and strength. Give unto the Lord the glory due unto his name; worship the Lord in the beauty of holiness.

One of my primary points was this truth—that the mightiest people in the world are those who have been given access into the throne room of God to petition Him in prayer. I ended the message talking about backslidden Samson—weak before his enemies, stripped of his glory, chained to a mill wheel, and mocked by his captors. In spite of all this he prayed, "O Lord God, remember me," and then he "bowed himself with *all his might*" (Judges 16:28, 30, kjv, emphasis added). I told the congregation, "I don't care how far you've fallen, how many mistakes you've made, how enslaved you may have become, or how far you feel from fulfilling your vision in life. Pray with all your might! Worship with all your might! Push against the pillars, the strongholds in your life, until they come crashing down. God did it for Samson. He will do it for you!"

Then it happened! About one hundred people ran to the altar, seeking to be renewed in their commitment to God and filled with the baptism of the Holy Spirit. Like wind-swept fire, supernatural power passed through the room as if God Himself were personally visiting us from another realm. There are no words to describe what we experienced. Almost everyone began effortlessly speaking in tongues as the Holy Spirit gave them utterance. The atmosphere was truly electrified with "joy unspeakable" (1 Pet. 1:8).

Then I looked at my watch. "Oh no," I thought, "it's 6:30. I'm supposed to stop this service so the next group can come in." It was a dilemma. I had promised the pastor to be sensitive to the schedule, or the parking lot would become an impossible, snarled mess. Yet I felt it would dishonor God to stop what was going on. Being a guest in another man's church, I intended to respectfully comply with His wishes. I looked over at Pastor Williams with a look of concern. Being a spiritual man, he knew what I was feeling and waved me on, mouthing the words, "Keep going." We did. The next group of one thousand people came in and stood for hours in an atmosphere that became increasingly saturated with celestial glory. Many more came to the altar and were baptized in the Holy Spirit. We lingered far into the night.

It was a move of God I will never forget. It all happened because we offered the Father not a cheap wicker chair of half-hearted praise but a golden throne of sincere, creative, passionate worship in which He could be "enthroned." This promise still hovers over every believer who seeks the face of God in sincerity and truth.

POWERFUL PROCLAMATION

I proclaim that my highest calling is worship. I am one of the *mighty* because the *Almighty* has given me the honor of accessing His presence. Even now I offer Him a throne of adoration in which He can seat Himself—radiating His authority, dominion, power, and rest into every corner of my life. Yes, God inhabits—He enthrones Himself—on the praise I send upward to Him. *This is God's promise to me. I claim this supernatural impartation and expect its manifestation in my life.*

Additional Insights: Psalm 100:1–5;
Matthew 21:1–11; Acts 16:16–40; Hebrews 10:19–22

SPIRITUAL WEAPONS

For the weapons of our warfare are not carnal, but mighty through God to the pulling down of strongholds.

—2 Corinthians 10:4

S PIRITUAL WARFARE IS the nature of this world. It intensifies the moment a child of darkness surrenders to Jesus, the captain of our salvation, and becomes a child of light. From that point the battle is on to reclaim the redeemed and delivered one. Two opposing kingdoms—the kingdom of light and the kingdom of darkness—constantly collide with each other, vying for control of our lives. Often the arena of conflict is the mind. Thankfully God has given a strong promise.

> For though we walk in the flesh, we do not war according to the flesh. For the weapons of our warfare are not carnal, but mighty through God to the pulling down of strongholds, casting down imaginations and every high thing that exalts itself against the knowledge of God, bringing every thought into captivity to the obedience of Christ.
>
> —2 Corinthians 10:3–5

The primary pledge in this passage is that believers have God-given "weapons" that are capable of "pulling down strongholds." These strongholds are areas of persistent wrong thinking that dominate the mind. They are the result of things such as intellectual coercion, abuse, false doctrine, harmful attitudes, sinful behavior choices, or demonic deception.

This passage does not emphasize fighting demons directly, but rather overcoming negative thought processes of the fallen Adamic nature—human imagination that exalts itself against true revelation. However, it is true that these things can become open doors for demonic infestation, especially in situations such as addictions, false religious practices, or persistent immorality.

Once our minds are brought under the power of the One who said, "I am…the truth," beliefs and behavior patterns should change so that demons lose access into our minds, hearts, and lives (John 14:6). A "spiritual mind" is not something we have to plead to obtain; it is a gift from God. We who are saved have been given "the mind of Christ" (1 Cor. 2:16). We should thank God for the daily manifestation of this supernatural resource of divine knowledge and wisdom.

We have many weapons in our spiritual arsenal. Every God-given character trait infused into our spirits is a weapon against its negative, evil opposite. For instance, the joy of the Lord is a weapon against depression, the love of God is a weapon against hate, the wisdom of the Highest is a weapon against foolishness, and divine righteousness, poured into our hearts, is a weapon against wickedness.

These are all inseparably attached to our three primary weapons:

+ The Word of God
+ The blood of Jesus
+ The name of the Lord

GOD'S POWER RELEASED IN AN ASYLUM

I have seen the power of these weapons demonstrated thousands of times in overcoming strongholds, but one experience tops them all. It happened in upstate New York where I was scheduled to preach at a Church of God. After driving all day from Tennessee, I arrived at about six o'clock at night. When I knocked on the door of the pastor's home, he abruptly walked out of the house, locked the door, and announced, "I'm glad you're here. Let's go."

Surprised, I asked, "Where are we headed?"

He responded, "The insane asylum," and left me hanging with no explanation.

In a dry attempt at humor, I said, "Do you treat all your visiting evangelists this way?" He smiled wryly and proceeded to explain. The head of his intercessory team was a seasoned saint of God who was unfortunately married to a verbally abusive man. He constantly harassed her, telling her how stupid, ugly, and worthless she was. Though she had fended off his demeaning accusations for many years, for some reason, a few weeks before I arrived, she finally succumbed to the pressure and suffered a mental collapse.

When we arrived at the asylum, it was near closing time. They reluctantly gave us five minutes to visit but cautioned us against doing anything "religious." We smiled non-confrontationally and proceeded to her room, expecting God to move.

She seemed to be in another world—crouched in the middle of the bed, staring into space, constantly muttering about how stupid, ugly, and worthless she was. (Apparently she finally believed the lies.) She was completely dysfunctional: never bathing herself, clothing herself, or feeding herself. She didn't even acknowledge us being in the room.

The pastor kindly motioned for me to take the lead. Even though she acted totally oblivious to anything I said, I felt that in her subconscious mind, she heard and comprehended my words. I took up "the sword of the Spirit, which is the word of God" (Eph. 6:17). Facing off with the enemy the same way Jesus did in the wilderness with Satan, I got close to one side of her head and began quoting every power promise that came to my mind—reinforcing it by saying, "It is written."

- It is written, "Behold, I give unto you power… over all the power of the enemy" (Luke 10:19, KJV).

- It is written, "Greater is he that is in you, than he that is in the world" (1 John 4:4, KJV).

- It is written, "If God be for us, who can be against us?" (Rom. 8:31, KJV).

- It is written, "There is therefore now no condemnation for those who are in Christ Jesus" (Rom. 8:1).

+ It is written, "The peace of God, which surpasses all understanding, will guard your hearts and minds through Christ Jesus" (Phil. 4:7, NKJV).

+ It is written, "For God has not given us a spirit of fear, but of power and of love and of a sound mind" (2 Tim. 1:7, NKJV).

And quite a few more.

Somewhat nervously I looked at my watch. Four minutes and thirty seconds had passed. It was almost time to go. We only had about thirty seconds left. I blurted out, "Pastor, we better go for it!" We both laid hands on her simultaneously, claimed the blood of Jesus, declared the power of His name, and spoke in tongues with all our might.

Unfortunately two big, muscular "bouncers" had been listening just outside the door. When they heard things escalate, they rushed in, grabbed us by the arms, and rudely escorted us to the front door, throwing us out in the yard and locking the doors behind us. It mattered little. We had already done sufficient damage to the devil's stronghold.

As soon as they removed us from her room, that daughter of God got up, took a shower, and clothed herself. Then she went up to the front desk and said, "Call my family to come get me. I don't need to be in here anymore." That week, she attended the conference and told her story. We were all reminded once again of the powerful spiritual promise "No weapon that is formed against you shall prosper" (Isa. 54:17).

POWERFUL PROCLAMATION

I proclaim that I have the mind of Christ. I am filled with His infinite knowledge and wisdom. God has not given me the spirit of fear but of power, and of love, and of a sound mind. By the weapons of warfare that He has given me (the blood of Jesus, the name of Jesus, and the Word of God), I take authority over every evil imagination and every negative attitude that would exalt itself against the true revelation of God's Word. Those strongholds must fall by the power of God. *This is God's promise to me. I claim this supernatural impartation and expect its manifestation in my life.*

Additional Insights: Genesis 6:5–7, KJV;
Isaiah 26:3; Jeremiah 31:33; Matthew 4:1–11

YOU MAY ALL PROPHESY

For you may all prophesy one by one, that all may learn and all may be encouraged.

—1 CORINTHIANS 14:31

DURING ISRAEL'S JOURNEY through the Wilderness of Sin, Moses prayed, "Oh, that all the people of the LORD were prophets, and that the LORD would put His Spirit upon them!" (Num. 11:29). That prayer was answered with the coming of the new covenant.

On the day of Pentecost, when the wind of heaven blew in the Upper Room and the fire of God fell, the early disciples were baptized in the power of the Holy Spirit. Then they "began to speak with other tongues, as the Spirit gave them utterance," preaching in various languages about "the wonderful works of God" (Acts 2:4, 11, NKJV).

Then Peter stood up and preached the first sermon of the new covenant era, explaining how an ancient prophecy had just been fulfilled:

For these are not drunk, as you suppose, since it is the third hour of the day. But this is what was spoken by the prophet Joel: "In the last days it shall be," says God, "that I will pour out My Spirit on all flesh; your sons and your daughters shall prophesy, your young men shall see visions, and your old men shall dream dreams. Even on

My menservants and maidservants I will pour out My
Spirit in those days; and they shall prophesy."

—Acts 2:15–18

According to this passage, not just a few but *all* sons and
daughters of God in this era (*all* "menservants and maidservants") are anointed to prophesy. How can that be? Isn't
the gift of prophecy reserved for a select group of believers?
That depends on how you define the term. There are three
distinct levels to the prophetic:

+ **The first level:** In its simplest form, prophesying
  is sharing God's Word under the power of the
  Holy Spirit. Because true believers are begotten
  of the Word and born of the Spirit, when they
  talk about the Bible, on a basic level they are
  prophesying—for the Word of God and the
  Spirit of God flow out of them. When they share
  the steps of salvation with those who do not
  know the Lord, they prophetically open a door
  into future glory, even the glory of eternal life.
  For this reason Revelation 19:10 states that "the
  testimony of Jesus is the spirit of prophecy."

+ **The second level:** When Bible believers reveal
  the future of this world by declaring biblical
  prophecies that have already been spoken by
  prophets of the old and new covenant eras, they
  are prophesying on the second level. They are not
  initiating these prophetic insights but echoing
  what has already been established.

+ **The third level:** Though any true Christian can be used this way, this third level is most evidenced in leaders who are called to the office of a prophet (one of fivefold ministry leadership callings mentioned in Ephesians 4:11). It occurs when God initiates through such individuals unique, prophetic words, either by instantaneous utterances, impulses from the Holy Spirit, dreams, or visions.

Paul urged all the Corinthian church members to pursue the manifestations of the Holy Spirit. He exhorted them to "follow after love and desire spiritual gifts, but especially that you may prophesy" (1 Cor. 14:1). Then, in verse 31, he boldly projected, "For you may all prophesy one by one, that all may learn and all may be encouraged."

Yes, God includes all His people, but if we fail to identify with this prophetic role, we may never walk in it. We could end up either ignoring or denying our potential inheritance. As we go through each day, we should praise God in expectation that the river of the prophetic will flow out of our innermost being—that God will give us intuitive insights and inspired words in all our encounters—and that we will dare to act on what we feel.

RESPONDING PROPHETICALLY
IN CHALLENGING TIMES

The prophetic often occurs when believers are not consciously pursuing it. God "interrupts" the thought processes. When it happens this way, it is all the more certain that the insights are divinely inspired. One of the greatest examples I could share concerns my wife, Elizabeth. She was five months pregnant with our daughter. We were at a routine doctor's appointment when he led us to a video screen to show us the result of an ultrasound test. Glumly he projected, "Your daughter has spina bifida" (a hole in the spine). She will probably never walk." He also claimed she had cretinism (severe retardation). Then he had the audacity, knowing we were ministers, to offer "an alternative" (a softer word for abortion, which is murder). We were so offended for the Lord's sake and for our child's sake that we jumped up to leave, never intending to return.

As we walked down the hall, Elizabeth was broken-hearted and distraught. Then suddenly she heard the audible voice of God prophesying, "Your daughter will dance on the streets of Jerusalem!" What God said was totally opposite of what the doctor proposed.

When we got in the car, Jesus verified the prophetic word in a very peculiar way (as He often does). Still tense from what we had faced, Elizabeth turned on the radio just to calm her nerves, and the song that came on was "I Hope You Dance" by Lee Ann Womack. Stunned, my wife turned to me and said, "It's a confirmation of what I just heard." Then she shared the revelation with me that she had just received from God.

From that day forward—many times during the entire pregnancy—Elizabeth laid hands on her belly, making prophetic declarations over our baby girl. She often quoted Psalm 138:8 (NKJV): "The LORD will perfect that which concerns me," and then she would decree, "Little baby, you concern me, so I declare that you are perfect." After that she would sing, "I Hope You Dance."

Months before her birth we named our child Destiny Hope to counteract the negative statements of the doctor who had forecast a somewhat hopeless future for her. We understood that these are things you prayerfully do to function on a prophetic level. It worked. When Destiny came forth from the womb, the first thing the attending doctor said was, "She's perfect." And at an early age she also displayed a passion for dance.

We received our miracle, most likely because we did something Paul admonished Timothy to do. We waged a "good warfare" by declaring the prophetic word that had been spoken over us (1 Tim. 1:18, NKJV). Go ahead, prophets and prophetesses, speak as "oracles of God" and fight the good fight of faith (1 Pet. 4:11).

> The lion has roared; who will not fear? The Lord GOD has spoken; who can but prophesy?
> —AMOS 3:8

POWERFUL PROCLAMATION

I proclaim that I have been begotten of the Word and born of the Spirit. By this dual internal influence I can speak prophetically into the lives of those I meet every day and into my own life. I also believe the Holy Spirit will grant me flashes of insight concerning biblical truth and concerning people and situations so that I might help and inspire others with the help and the inspiration I receive from God. I am commissioned and empowered to share the testimony of Jesus, which is the spirit of prophecy. *This is God's promise to me. I claim this supernatural impartation and expect its manifestation in my life.*

Additional Insights: Numbers 12:6;
Ezekiel 37:1–14; Romans 12:6

PROMISE 17

DREAMS FROM GOD

In a dream, in a vision of the night, when deep sleep falls upon men, in slumber on their beds, then He opens the ears of men, and seals their instruction.

—JOB 33:15–16

T HE VOICE OF the almighty God that thundered from Mount Sinai also subtly whispers to the subconscious minds of people in the mysterious language of dreams. Filled with detailed imagery and profound symbolism, dreams are often an intriguing, poetical means the Creator uses to communicate truth.

When Peter preached the first sermon of the new covenant era on the day of Pentecost, he mentioned that this method of divine communication would be a dominant characteristic of this age of grace. Quoting from the prophet Joel, he shouted to the crowd that had gathered below the Upper Room.

> "In the last days it shall be," says God, "that I will pour out My Spirit on all flesh; your sons and your daughters shall prophesy, your young men shall see visions, and your old men shall dream dreams."
>
> —ACTS 2:17

Of course there are no age or gender barriers in the kingdom of God. Inspired dreams are not just reserved for "old men." People of all ages are candidates for these divinely authored means of communication. In Numbers 12:6 God said, "If there is a prophet among you, I the LORD will make Myself known to him in a vision, and I will speak to him in a dream." Because all new covenant sons and daughters are called to walk in the prophetic (on at least one of three levels), all should expect to receive dreams from God. (See promise 16, "You May All Prophesy.")

Various Bible characters were given powerful, God-inspired dreams, even some who were not in a covenant relationship with God. Let's look at a few.

- **Abimelech:** The king of Gerar was warned in a dream not to take Sarah as his wife because she was married to Abraham. (See Genesis 20:3–6.)

- **Jacob:** This son of Isaac had a dream of a ladder extending from earth to heaven, with angels ascending and descending on it and the Lord standing at the top uttering covenant promises. (See Genesis 28:10–22.)

- **Joseph:** This son of Jacob received two dreams revealing his future relationship with his parents and his eleven brothers. The dream-giver used the symbolism of eleven sheaves of wheat bowing to Joseph's sheaf, and in the second dream, the sun, moon, and eleven stars bowing to his star. (See Genesis 37:5–11.)

- **Pharaoh's chief baker and chief butler (his "cupbearer"):** Both of these distinguished individuals in Pharaoh's household received highly symbolic dreams from God (one involving a basket of baked goods; the other, a vine with ripe grapes). The details of these dreams were interpreted by Joseph, foretelling that one would be executed and the other would be restored to his position. (See Genesis 40.)

+ **Pharaoh:** God gave Pharaoh two successive, related dreams of what the future held for the people of that region. Seven fine-looking, fattened cows were devoured by seven gaunt and ugly cows, and then seven plump and good heads of grain were devoured by seven thin and blighted heads of grain. Both dreams signified a seven-year period of abundance devoured by the ravages of a seven-year famine. (See Genesis 41:1–36.)

+ **Solomon:** The Lord appeared to Solomon in a dream at night, and He said, "Ask what you want from Me." Solomon unselfishly asked for wisdom to lead God's people, which God granted, but He added, "I have also given you what you have not asked, both riches and honor, so that no kings will compare to you all of your days" (1 Kings 3:5, 13).

+ **Nebuchadnezzar:** The king of Babylon dreamed of a great image made of gold, silver, bronze, iron, and clay, which represented five dominant empires emerging in the earth. At the climax of the dream a stone cut out without hands fell on the image and crushed it, and then it grew into a great mountain that filled the earth. The stone was a symbol of the Messiah at His second coming. (See Daniel 2.)

+ **Joseph:** Mary's husband-to-be was deeply disappointed because she was found to be with child before their marriage. "But while he thought on these things, the angel of the Lord appeared to him in a dream saying, 'Joseph, son of David, do not be afraid to take Mary as your wife, for He who is conceived in her is of the Holy Spirit'" (Matt. 1:20). Thus a dream from God introduced the Messiah to the world.

These examples prove that God often uses divinely inspired dreams to direct and promote His purposes in this world. I can testify on a personal level that inspired dreams have guided my life for nearly fifty years.

A Pivotal Insight From God

Years ago I was in a quandary concerning the will of God. My open-air crusades in India had been extremely fruitful, with thousands of precious Hindu people experiencing true salvation. I wanted to remain there and devote the rest of my life to impacting that populous nation with the gospel, but I just could not feel a release. I even spent an entire day fasting and praying on top of a mountain in India, pleading with God for direction—but heaven was silent.

Still in turmoil over the matter, I returned to the United States, resigning myself over to what I felt would be a far more meager harvest of souls. Driving to one of my first evangelistic meetings back home, I decided to take a break, park my van in a McDonald's parking lot, and spend some time in prayer. Closing the curtains in front and kneeling in the back, I started seeking God. Twenty or thirty minutes went by, and then unintentionally I fell asleep on my knees. Immediately I was carried away in the Spirit—in an inspired dream—and God showed me His purpose in bringing me back to the United States.

I saw an outline of the United States and a little red dot in the heart of America, positioned about where Cleveland, Tennessee, is—the city where I reside. Suddenly that red dot exploded into two blood-red words, one superimposed on the other, flowing into the whole map of America until every community was saturated with the precious blood of the Messiah. Those two blood-red words were "JESUS SAVES!"

I immediately understood what God was saying. First, it concerned my own ministry, that my work was to primarily be in my own country and culture; but second and most importantly, it was a revelation that we will see another great awakening in the United States—one that will impact every community, one that I believe will exceed the Jesus movement and the Charismatic movement combined, border to border and coast to coast. I feel certain this will come to pass in our generation. The need is greater than ever. The rise in witchcraft, false cults, atheism, immorality, and perversity has deepened the darkness, but the God who gives dreams will bring it to pass.

POWERFUL PROCLAMATION

I proclaim that my heavenly Father often communicates to His people by means of inspired dreams. I believe that He will speak to me this way and that He will also give me the wisdom to correctly interpret the heaven-sent dreams I receive. *This is God's promise especially to His people in this new covenant era. I claim this supernatural impartation and expect its manifestation in my life.*

Additional Insights: Judges 7:1–15;
Jeremiah 23:28; Daniel 4; Matthew 2:19–23; 27:11–19

SIGNS AND WONDERS

*See, I and the children whom the LORD has given
me are for signs and for wonders in Israel from
the LORD of Hosts who dwells in Mount Zion.*

—ISAIAH 8:18

INITIALLY THIS PROMISE was fulfilled through the prophet Isaiah. When his children were born, he gave them prophetic names that foretold two major events soon to unfold (Shear-jashub, meaning a remnant shall return, and Maher-shalal-hash-baz, meaning quick to the plunder). These were descriptions of what would happen after the Northern Kingdom of Israel attacked the Southern Kingdom of Judah, carrying many captives away (a remnant returned), and how afterward the empire of Assyria invaded the Northern Kingdom as a judgment from God. (They were quick to the plunder; see Isaiah 7–8.)

According to Hebrews 2:13, this verse also speaks, on a much higher level, of the children of God under the new covenant. It's as if the Messiah Himself is speaking, declaring that all His spiritual offspring in this era are called to be "signs" and "wonders" in the earth.

+ A sign is usually something natural and visible that represents something spiritual and invisible, such as the rainbow representing God's promise

not to send a global flood again. A sign can also
be an extraordinary, supernatural happening
from God that confirms and validates a certain
truth, prophecy, or spokesperson.

+ A wonder is a miraculous event that causes those
who see it to be filled with worshipful awe as they
recognize God's greatness.

At pivotal points in history God has manifested signs
and wonders to verify His involvement in the affairs of His
people. One of the greatest examples is how God effected
the deliverance of the children of Israel from Egypt by a
series of "signs and wonders" (Deut. 6:22). Since that time,
God has continued to confirm His love for His own by
manifesting Himself in miraculous ways, for our Redeemer
is "the same yesterday, and today, and forever" (Heb. 13:8).

When the Savior came into this world, Simeon, the
prophet, held the incarnate God in his arms and announced
that He would be a "sign" that would be "spoken against"
(Luke 2:34). Apparently he meant that the Son of God was
a sign of a drastic change in the way God would deal with
those who come to Him for salvation. During His time
of ministry Jesus was "a Man attested by God...by *miracles, wonders, and signs*" (Acts 2:22, NKJV, emphasis added).
That's how the new covenant was introduced into the world.

After Jesus's ascension into heaven the persecuted early
church prayed for supernatural manifestations.

Now, Lord, look on their threats and grant that Your
servants may speak Your word with great boldness, by

stretching out Your hand to heal and that signs and wonders may be performed in the name of Your holy Son Jesus.

—Acts 4:29–30

God answered that prayer in the first century, and He is still stretching out His hand to do mighty things in our era.

God Thwarts a Murderous Plot

One of the greatest examples of this promise being fulfilled in my ministry happened in an outdoor evangelistic campaign I conducted in Kumbakonam, India. According to the pastoral committee sponsoring the meeting, I was the first Western missionary to conduct such a meeting within the city limits. About five thousand attended.

Hindu people are normally very gentle and tolerant, but that night six radical Hindus decided to do whatever was necessary to stop Christian evangelistic efforts in their city. They planned to storm the platform, beat me up publicly, tie me to the bumper of their car, and drag me through their city. Thankfully the God of signs and wonders had a different plan.

Toward the end of my message that night I sensed that if I gave an invitation, few would respond. Many had just been exposed to the gospel for the first time, and I could sense that they did not fully comprehend what they heard. Then God spoke to my heart, "Call for the deaf...and tell the crowd that if what you have preached was correct, every one of them will hear again."

Trembling, I obeyed. Little did I know how important my choice would be, not only to them but to me personally. After I challenged the audience, seven deaf persons were brought forward to the platform. Four were totally deaf, and three, deaf in only one ear. I intentionally chose one who was totally deaf first—a twenty-four-year-old who had lost his hearing five years before.

Just as I began to pray, everyone on the platform became very distracted by a loud, slamming, bashing sound behind us. Six radical Hindus had crept up the stairwell and were hitting the large padlock on a twenty-foot-high gate over and over to break in. The padlock finally burst and fell to the concrete. Immediately the gate swung open, and the men came running toward me. As I turned to see, the young man I was praying for jerked out of my hands and began leaping for joy, shouting to the audience that he could hear. The crowd erupted in excitement—but the leader of the radical group stopped and stared at the young man, shaking his head in amazement.

Then he walked over and whispered into his ears to test if he could really hear. After the young man repeated his words back, he called his associates over, and they too tested to see if he was truly healed. They began to talk among themselves, saying things such as, "A miracle has truly happened!" Not knowing the men had come to harm me, I continued praying for the other six deaf people, until all were hearing again perfectly.

Since God fulfilled the challenge, I made an altar call, and hundreds came forward, giving their lives to Jesus (including the six men who intended to disrupt the meeting). It was the next day before I learned of their original intentions (when they requested to meet with me). I also found out the real reason the leader did not follow through with his plan—the first deaf person healed was his next-door neighbor. What a divinely orchestrated connection! God manifested a sign and a wonder that proved the gospel to an audience of people who knew little or nothing about it, but He worked an even greater miracle in preventing my death.

Of course this story is an extreme example. In far more subtle ways God uses His people as signs and wonders every day. As we walk in joy and hope, we become a sign that depression and discouragement can be conquered. As we walk in Christian love and forgiveness, we become a sign that there is a solution to a hate-filled, prejudiced, war-racked world. When others consider our past and the great transformation that has been wrought in our lives, they "wonder" how the God of heaven could be so personally involved in a fallen human race. Yes, in myriad ways every day we fulfill this role of being signs and wonders in the earth.

POWERFUL PROCLAMATION

I proclaim that God has made me a sign and a wonder. The supernatural transformation of my life is a sign to others that God can intervene in their lives as well. I expect to be a source of truth for those in deception, a source of hope for those who despair, a source of faith for those who doubt, a source of peace for those who are anxious, a source of forgiveness for those who are bitter, and a source of love for those who feel despised. I declare that people around me will be filled with wonder at the greatness of God because of the wondrous things He does in me. *This is God's promise to me. I claim this supernatural impartation and expect its manifestation in my life.*

Additional Insights: Psalm 71:7;
Acts 2:17–19; Hebrews 2:3–4; Revelation 12:1

MOVING MOUNTAINS

Jesus answered them, "Have faith in God. For truly I say to you, whoever says to this mountain, 'Be removed and be thrown into the sea,' and does not doubt in his heart, but believes that what he says will come to pass, he will have whatever he says."

—**MARK 11:22–23**

THIS MOUNTAIN-MOVING PROMISE is one of the weightiest propositions in the teachings of Jesus (no pun intended). Most likely it was intentional exaggeration. (No one—not even the Son of God Himself—has ever literally ripped a mountain out of the ground with the spoken word.) It was a metaphor, a word-picture meant to illustrate a powerful and important concept by connecting it to an unforgettable mental image.

You see, there is nothing more immovable, unchangeable, or intimidating than a lofty mountain, so it represents the most immovable, unchangeable, and intimidating situations you could ever face in life—both oppositions and challenges. (You may be thinking right now, you're not dealing with one mountain but an entire mountain range. If so, this promise is *definitely for you*.)

An obscure passage from the Old Testament is a good starting point.

Zerubbabel, the newly installed governor of Jerusalem, was faced with the prospect of rebuilding the destroyed temple. The Jews had just returned from seventy years of bondage in Babylon. Brokenness—their holy city, Jerusalem, was in ruins. Deep sorrow—the temple mount was a garbage heap. Overwhelmed—what Zerubbabel and his associates must have felt in the privacy of their own hearts.

Then, the prophet Haggai made a stupendous claim and tagged God to it.

> Who is left among you who saw this house in its former glory? How do you see it now? Is it not, in your eyes, as nothing in comparison?... The glory of this latter house will be greater than the former, says the Lord of Hosts.
>
> —Haggai 2:3, 9

Zerubbabel must have pondered, "How could such a thing ever come to pass? The temple was the most glorious building ever constructed in Israel. The Shekinah glory of God swept into it so mightily, the priests could not even stand up to minister. What could exceed that?"

Zechariah, another prophet during that same era, gave the governor an important key.

> This is the word of the Lord to Zerubbabel: "Not by might nor by power, but by My Spirit," says the Lord of hosts. "Who are you, O great mountain? Before Zerubbabel you shall become a plain! And he shall bring forth the capstone with shouts of 'Grace, grace to it!'"
>
> —Zechariah 4:6–7, nkjv

It happened. The temple was rebuilt. Though initially inferior to the first, centuries later, under Herod, the latter house became larger than Solomon's original temple. But what was the "greater glory"? Could it have been the Lord of glory Himself (God manifested in the flesh) walking in the temple area and teaching the mysteries of the kingdom? What could be more glorious than that?

And so begins the biblical tradition of speaking to mountains.

Maybe you should try speaking to your mountain the same way. First, name your mountain. Envision it. Announce what it represents. Then dare to say, "Who are you, O great mountain? Before _____ (insert your name) you will become a plain!"

Did you feel that surge of confidence?

Another great passage from Isaiah, the prophet, is a well-known prophecy of the coming of Jesus.

> The voice of one crying in the wilderness: "Prepare the way of the LORD; make straight in the desert a highway for our God. Every valley shall be exalted and every mountain and hill brought low; the crooked places shall be made straight and the rough places smooth.
> —ISAIAH 40:3–4, NKJV; SEE LUKE 3:1–6

The "one crying in the wilderness" was John the Baptist. The "highway" he prepared in the desert was his message of repentance that prepared the hearts of the Israelites for the Promised One. During the Messiah's short life span of thirty-three years every mountain—every dark,

towering, unbeatable, unconquerable foe in this world—
was "brought low."

Through His torturous death and glorious resurrection
huge, overpowering "Mount Everest-sized" summits—such
as the curse of separation from God, the curse of the sin
nature, and the curse of death—in one day were ripped
from the ground and thrown into the sea. A tsunami of
change swept across the world from that point onward. In
anticipation of this global reach God also promised in the
very next verse, "The glory of the LORD shall be revealed,
and all flesh shall see it together" (Isa. 40:5).

Before the Son of God gave this supreme example,
though, while He was yet on the earth, He made sure
His followers understood this mountain-moving calling—
by teaching them in the classroom of the real world. The
father of an epileptic boy brought his son to the disciples
for healing, but they were unable to set him free. When
Jesus heard what happened, in strong language He rebuked
His disciples.

> O faithless and perverse generation, how long shall I be
> with you? How long shall I bear with you? Bring him
> here to Me.
> —MATTHEW 17:17

When Jesus cast out the demon, the child was delivered
instantly. The disciples, embarrassed and frustrated over
their failure, asked why they could not heal the boy. Jesus
responded,

Because of your unbelief. For truly I say to you, if you have faith as a grain of mustard seed, you will say to this mountain, "Move from here to there," and it will move. And nothing will be impossible for you.

—MATTHEW 17:20

Faith like a grain of mustard seed? That's about two millimeters thick (one-twelfth of an inch). This means it only takes a little faith. In some cases time is also required for faith to do its work. (Mustard seeds must be planted in the ground and germinate and have time to grow.)

If you have this amazing gift called faith, "nothing will be impossible for you." (Chew on that truth until you can swallow it.)

Potential mountain movers need to remember the two conditions revealed in our theme scripture at the beginning:

1. You cannot doubt in your heart (even if you fight doubts in your mind).
2. You must believe what you say will come to pass (and don't work against yourself by speaking the opposite).

Then Jesus added, "Whatever things you ask when you pray, believe that you will receive them, and you will have them" (Mark 11:24). How? By praising God as if the answer is already in motion.

Wishful thinking? Or does this really work? I know it works. The skeptics have come too late to dissuade me. I have irrefutable evidence.

An Amazing, Creative Miracle

The little prayer group in Tampa, Florida, that prayed me into the kingdom of God was a breeding ground for miracles. One of the greatest acts of divine intervention in its history happened for seven-year-old Benjamin Godwin, the youngest son of two prominent members of the church, Les and Sylvia Godwin.

Ben was riding his bicycle one day when he was hit by a car, initially throwing him up on the hood of the car and mangling the bike underneath. Then, when the driver slammed on his brakes, Ben was thrown to the pavement. When he tried to stand to his feet, his left leg collapsed like an accordion underneath him. At first he was unaware that a three-inch piece of his shinbone had been dislodged, splintered beyond repair. It was lying on the pavement in a pool of blood.

It took three surgeries just to clean the wound. The surgeon told Ben's parents that even with numerous operations, including bone grafts, they would never be able to fully repair the break. Their boy would always walk with a noticeable limp. Ben's leg was placed in a full-length cast, with pins above and beneath the gap to hold the remaining bones in place. Everyone anticipated a very long journey to partial recovery and no hope for normalcy ever again—everyone, that is, except Pastor Bertha Madden, Ben's parents, and the Faith Pool Prayer Group at the House of Hope.

During one of its Friday night prayer meetings, Sister Madden began weeping in compassion for Ben. Trembling in intercession, she crawled across the room on her knees and laid hands on his cast. Then she uttered a mountain-moving faith decree with divine authority in her voice: "A new bone for Ben! O, God, honor Your Word with a new bone in this leg."

Ben felt a jerk inside his cast. Excitedly he told his parents that he was almost certain God had healed him. X-rays confirmed soon after, there were three inches of brand new bone in his leg.

Because of that amazing creative miracle, Ben never did limp; in fact, he was a star athlete in high school. During that same period, he was baptized in the Holy Spirit in one of my evangelistic meetings. He received a total transformation, both physical and spiritual—and all because believers surrounding him dared to pray in faith in the face of disaster. Though Pastor Madden didn't word it this way, she could have easily said:

"Who are you, O great mountain? Before the Faith Pool Prayer Group, by the power of the name of Jesus, you shall become a plain."[1]

Now it's your turn. Fear not. Believe. Declare. Decree. The God of creative miracles still lives.

POWERFUL PROCLAMATION

I proclaim that I have faith as a grain of mustard seed. It is alive and growing. God's Word urges me to speak against the mountains in my life. I refuse to doubt. I identify those mountains and believe with all my heart, "In the name of Jesus, you must move." I believe that what I say will come to pass. God will honor His Word. *This is God's promise to me. I claim this supernatural impartation and expect its manifestation in my life.*

Additional Insights: Isaiah 41:10–17;
Matthew 21:18–21; Mark 11:12–24

Promise 20

THE PROMISE OF THE FATHER

Being assembled with them, He commanded them, "Do not depart from Jerusalem, but wait for the promise of the Father, of which you have heard from Me. For John baptized with water, but you shall be baptized with the Holy Spirit not many days from now."

—Acts 1:4–5

THE VERSE ABOVE was part of the last recorded conversation Jesus had with His disciples before ascending into heaven. Ten days later it happened. The Holy Spirit came into the Upper Room like a rushing, mighty wind. Then tongues of fire appeared over their heads. Wind and fire—two of the most unpredictable and uncontrollable forces of nature—were heaven's emblems on that grand and glorious day.

Together they double in strength. A windswept fire can do enormous damage—and so it was with the wind and fire that came from above, yet in a positive sense. It swept through Israel and into the Gentile world, consuming the combustible material of repentant men and women who inclined their hearts toward heaven. The dark kingdom of the adversary was devastated as the new covenant burned out of control, effecting a massive paradigm shift in the earth spiritually.

The final statement of the Messiah in this passage was both a prophetic promise and a challenging commission.

> But you shall receive power when the Holy Spirit comes upon you. And you shall be My witnesses in Jerusalem, and in all Judea and Samaria, and to the ends of the earth.
>
> —ACTS 1:8

"The promise of the Father" was not just about receiving; it was about becoming—becoming God's representatives in the earth to declare the truth amid falsehood, empowered to bring change to people's lives.

Right after the Holy Spirit fell in the Upper Room, Peter stood up and made a proclamation to the crowd that had gathered.

> Repent and be baptized, every one of you, in the name of Jesus Christ for the forgiveness of sins, and you shall receive the gift of the Holy Spirit. For the promise is to you, and to your children, and to all who are far away, as many as the Lord our God will call.
>
> —ACTS 2:38–39

What did Peter mean by the "promise"?

One simple word, yet so profound, so powerful, so pivotal. To understand, we need to visit four ancient oracles who saw this glorious era in advance.

THE ANCIENT ORACLES

Four Old Testament prophets—Jeremiah, Ezekiel, Joel, and Malachi—gave us keys that unlock the door of this mystery. Other prophets were mightily used in pointing to this era too, but these are the four primary voices I will quote concerning what happened on Pentecost.

+ Jeremiah foretold that God would make a "new covenant" with His people containing three main elements: the law would be written in their hearts, they would all know Him personally, and their sins would be remembered no more. (See Jeremiah 31:31–34.)

+ Ezekiel foretold that God would "cleanse" His people and that He would give them "a new heart" and "a new spirit," taking out of them the "stony heart" (of prideful rebellion against God) and placing within them "a heart of flesh" (a submissive and sensitive heart). Most importantly God promised to place His Spirit within His people and cause them to walk in His statutes. (See Ezekiel 36:25–27.)

+ Joel foretold that in the last days God would pour out His Spirit on all flesh (both Jews and Gentiles) and that it would be a time when dreams, visions, and prophesying would abound among His people, an age when "wonders" would happen in the earth. (See Joel 2:28–30.)

+ Malachi revealed that the Messiah would be the "Messenger of the covenant," that He would be like "a refiner's fire and like launderers' soap," that He would "purify" His people and be "the Sun of Righteousness" arising "with healing in His wings"—over those blessed persons who fear His name (Mal. 3:1–3; 4:2, NKJV).

Later, when Jesus interceded over the church in John 17, He prayed that once He was glorified, His people would be kept from the evil one and sanctified by the truth, He would dwell in their hearts, they would be with Him where He is, and much more. (See John 17.) These wonderful commitments should also be included because the Father always answers the intercession of the Son.

When all these divine pledges are combined (from the prophets and the Son of God), they make up "the promise": a singular "promise" made up of many promises. Like a multifaceted diamond, it radiates the brilliant light of truth into every part of our lives and every part of our being. What does it take to receive "the promise"?

It is so utterly simple—Peter pledged that in this era, "everyone who calls on the name of the LORD will be saved" (Joel 2:32). Just uttering the beautiful name of Jesus brings heaven down to earth for those who believe. At that moment of salvation we are "sealed with the Holy Spirit of promise" (Eph. 1:13, NKJV). From that point forward we can be just as bold as Paul the apostle in declaring:

> The Lord will deliver me from every evil work and will preserve me for His heavenly kingdom, to whom be glory forever and ever. Amen.
>
> —2 Timothy 4:18

ATTRACTING GOD'S FIRE LIKE A LIGHTNING ROD

I will never forget the day when I was endued with the power of the Holy Spirit. I was born again a year before. The Holy Spirit was dwelling within me, but I knew I lacked something. I never felt the presence of God, and the gifts of the Spirit did not operate in me. I was truly saved; I was changed, but there was no deep, supernatural reality in my life. Then it happened, when I least expected it.

Of all places, I was walking into the parking lot of a Dairy Kreme to buy a banana split. (That was before I got health-minded—LOL.) There happened to be a woman sitting at a concrete table next to the restaurant. I noticed immediately she was wearing a large metal back brace.

I had participated in numerous prayer meetings in which I pleaded with God to fill me with the baptism of the Holy Spirit (that enduement with power that came in the Upper Room). Others often prayed for me, but I always left frustrated and empty, wondering why God didn't pour out His power. Just a few days before, though, I had shaken off the depression and told the Lord that if I never spoke in tongues, if I never felt His power, if I never received a spiritual awakening of His gifts in my life, I would still serve Him with all my heart and win every person I could into the kingdom of God. I must have passed a test. It was no longer about me and my spiritual fulfillment. It was all about Him and about others.

With no thought for myself, I walked up to the woman, introduced myself as a believer, told her I believed in healing, and asked if I could pray. She smiled and said she would be happy to agree with me in prayer. I lifted my left hand to heaven, reached out my right hand to take hers, and began interceding. That's when a "suddenly" moment of divine impartation took place with no warning.

My raised left hand must have been like a lightning rod that attracted the lightning of heaven. *Intense* is too mild a word. The fire of God hit me in the palm of my hand and rushed down into my chest area, where it exploded with a joy that was overpowering. I know why Peter called it "unspeakable" joy (1 Pet. 1:8). It was heaven on earth. Then it felt like a river of liquid fire flowing out of my inner being as I began speaking in tongues with all my might: shouting, leaping, and dancing all over that Dairy Kreme parking lot. It was amazing. It was glorious. It happened when I wasn't even asking—yet it was most likely the result of all the asking that led up to that point, for Jesus did promise, "If you then, being evil, know how to give good gifts to your children, how much more will your heavenly Father give the Holy Spirit to those who ask Him?" (Luke 11:13).

In a sense the "promise of the Father" took a year to fully unfold in my life—yet truthfully the process is still unfolding, growing deeper with every passing day, and will reach its peak of expression at the coming of the Lord.

POWERFUL PROCLAMATION

I proclaim that I have received "the promise": I am a child of the new covenant, God has written His law in my heart, I know Him personally, and my sins will never be remembered. God has cleansed me, given me a new heart and a new spirit, and placed His Spirit inside of me. The Messiah is like a refiner's fire in my life, and I will come forth as gold. He is the Sun of Righteousness arising over me with healing in His wings, so I am healed: body, mind, soul, and spirit. My inheritance is an enduement with power to be one of God's witnesses in the earth. *This is God's promise to me. I claim this supernatural impartation and expect its manifestation in my life.*

Additional Insights: John 14:26; 16:7–15; Ephesians 1:13–14; 4:30

SPEAKING IN TONGUES: THE REST AND THE REFRESHING

For with stammering lips and another tongue He will speak to this people, to whom He said, "This is the rest with which You may cause the weary to rest," and, "This is the refreshing": yet they would not hear.

—ISAIAH 28:11–12, NKJV

IN 1 CORINTHIANS 14:21 Paul verified that this old-covenant prophecy was foretelling the new-covenant gift often referred to as "speaking in tongues." It accompanied the infilling of the Holy Spirit on the day of Pentecost, a supernatural sign to the Jews gathered in Jerusalem that Jesus was truly the Messiah. Here is the stunning account:

When the Day of Pentecost had fully come, they were all with one accord in one place. And suddenly there came a sound from heaven, as of a rushing mighty wind, and it filled the whole house where they were sitting. Then there appeared to them divided tongues, as of fire, and one sat upon each of them. And they were all filled with the Holy Spirit and began to speak with other tongues, as the Spirit gave them utterance.

And there were dwelling in Jerusalem Jews, devout men, from every nation under heaven. And when this sound occurred, the multitude came together, and were confused, because everyone heard them speak in his own language. Then they were all amazed and marveled, saying to one another, "Look, are not all these who speak Galileans? And how is it that we hear, each in our own language in which we were born?...speaking in our own tongues the wonderful works of God."

—Acts 2:1–11, nkjv

On that glorious day speaking in tongues manifested for the primary purpose of preaching to the Jews "the wonderful works" that God had just wrought (the resurrection of the Son of God and the introduction of the new covenant). However, later Paul described this gift as "various kinds of tongues" because there are several ways it manifests (1 Cor. 12:10).

VARIOUS KINDS OF TONGUES

A language of prayer

First Corinthians 14:2 explains "he who speaks in an unknown tongue does not speak to men, but to God. For no one understands him, although in the spirit, he speaks mysteries." Tongues can be a rapturous language of adoration that ascends from members of the earthly bride of Christ to the heavenly Bridegroom. A mysterious love language of the regenerated spirit, it transcends intellect (which is based in the soul) and is often accompanied by extreme joy. Paul explained, "What is it then? I will pray with the spirit, and I will pray with the understanding. I will sing with the spirit, and I will sing with the understanding" (v. 15). Strangely, though the meaning of the words is rarely understood, those who speak in tongues this way "give thanks well" (v. 17).

"The rest" and "the refreshing"

When we "pray in the Holy Spirit," we build ourselves up in our "most holy faith"—so it awakens confidence, trust, and power (Jude 20). It brings peace that passes understanding, an inward witness of the rest of God (Heb. 4:1–3). The "refreshing" it releases can be expressed many ways, including fresh creativity, fresh passion for service, fresh fire to pursue vision, fresh love for others—all these things and more come when we exercise the wonderful gift of tongues.

A message to be interpreted

Notice the Bible does not instruct us to "translate" the gift of tongues; it tells us to "interpret" (1 Cor. 14:27). One sentence in tongues may take a paragraph in English to interpret. Concerning this type of speaking with tongues, Paul exhorted, "If anyone speaks in an unknown tongue, let it be by two, or at the most by three, and each in turn, and let one interpret. But if there is no interpreter, let him remain silent in the church, and let him speak to himself and to God" (vv. 27–28). Paul was not forbidding believers to speak in tongues in church at all. He was explaining that if someone has a message in tongues and there is no one with the gift of interpretation, he should instead commune with God in such a way that he does not draw attention to himself in the assembly of believers.

If a whole group of believers speaking in tongues simultaneously in a worshipful way is wrong, God moved contrary to His own will in pouring out His Spirit on the household of Cornelius. (See Acts 10:44–48.) Peter did not ask for that visitation to happen. Cornelius did not ask. It was a sovereign act of God. No one was present of other languages (that we know of); no one gave a message that needed interpretation. It was simply an anointed outburst of Spirit-inspired adoration.

A common misconception

I have often heard believers claim that Christians should speak in tongues because the devil cannot understand what is being said. I contend that is an incorrect and illogical concept for two main reasons.

+ First, Satan is not with us constantly. He is not omnipresent. He is not monitoring every prayer each believer prays. To believe so is a wild distortion of the truth. There are over two billion Christians in the world. If the devil were the intimidating, overshadowing adversary most Christians imagine, intercepting all our prayer communications to thwart them, he would have to be consciously present in over two billion places at once, processing all these conversations simultaneously (requiring that he be omnipresent and omniscient). These are attributes that belong to God alone. The devil's demonic underlings

may surround the planet ubiquitously but not the
prince of darkness himself.

+ Second, Paul described this wonderful gift as
"tongues of men and of angels" (1 Cor. 13:1). We
know that the devil and his subordinate demons
are very familiar with all human languages. They
tempt English people in English, Spanish people
in Spanish, French people in French, and so on.
Also, these fallen angels were once inhabitants of
heaven, so we can assume they know the language
of angels. (See Isaiah 14:12–19; Ezekiel 28:12–19.)

Therefore, the power of speaking in tongues,
quite possibly, is the fact that Satan and his
satanic underlings *do understand* what is being
said. They are fully aware that it is not frail
human beings praying a halting prayer, but the
omnipotent Holy Spirit praying through them to
the Father in a spirit of absolute faith and irre-
sistible power. They must know such utterances
are unopposable, unstoppable, and unconquerable.

My Experience of Tongues

I have experienced all three manifestations of this founda-
tional gift of the Holy Spirit. The first time was about a
year after I was born again. (See my story in "The Promise
of the Father.") Now I pray in tongues almost every day.
Many times I have interpreted messages in tongues. Two
times I have spoken in a known language that was translated by someone present.

One of those incidents was in a prayer session I conducted with about nine Baptist youth leaders from all around the world at Ridgecrest Baptist Assembly, just east of Asheville, North Carolina. We had just gone through the scriptures in the Book of Acts that imply the baptism of the Holy Spirit always comes with the manifestation of speaking in tongues (Acts 2:1–6; 10:44–48; 19:1–7). They were all confused, saying, "We've been taught that when we got saved, we received the Holy Spirit by faith, and there is nothing left to ask for."

I responded that there is a difference between the abiding presence of the Holy Spirit that comes when a person is born again and the baptism of the Spirit, which is an enduement with power for service.

They said, "We are still not sure."

I suggested, "Let's pray and ask God for His wisdom."

As we all joined hands and started praying, the Holy Spirit moved on me, and I began speaking in tongues. A youth leader from Chile, who was standing next to me, started trembling noticeably. I thought I was scaring him, but then he blurted out, "You are speaking in my language, in my native dialect."

I got very excited then. I responded, "Please tell me what I am saying."

He responded, "You are saying, 'I am the Lord your God, and the words My servant has spoken are words of truth. Hear him.'"

Needless to say, that dissolved their concerns. We had a marvelous prayer meeting, and all nine were baptized in the Holy Spirit with the evidence of speaking in tongues.

Speaking in tongues, in all three of its manifestations, is still a relevant gift in this hour. All nine gifts of the Holy Spirit should be the object of our prayers as we ask God for their manifestation. (See 1 Corinthians 12:7–11.) They can be grouped into three divisions.

+ **Power gifts:** healing, the working of miracles, and faith
+ **Revelation gifts:** the word of wisdom, the word of knowledge, and discerning of spirits
+ **Utterance gifts:** prophecy, various kinds of tongues, and interpretation of tongues

All gifts have been bought with the blood of Jesus, and none are to be shunned. All should be sought. Those received should be valued as a sacred treasure in the life of a believer. Even though tongues is the least of the nine gifts of the Spirit, it is a wonderful starting point and is far more important than many believers realize. Remember, the promise is that "the manifestation of the Spirit is given to everyone for the common good," and Paul did clearly conclude: "I desire that you all speak in tongues" (1 Cor. 12:7; 14:5).

POWERFUL PROCLAMATION

I proclaim that the gifts of the Holy Spirit are available to all believers distributed according to the will of God. I praise God for all three expressions of the gift of tongues flowing from the depths of my heart. I also claim the rest of God and the supernatural refreshing that accompanies this gift, delivering me from all spiritual weariness. I expect to be built up in my most holy faith as I give thanks to God this excellent way. *This is God's promise to me. I claim this supernatural impartation and expect its manifestation in my life.*

Additional Insights: Mark 16:15–20;
Acts 19:1–7; 1 Corinthians 14

THE HEAD AND NOT THE TAIL

*The LORD will make you the head and not the
tail; you will only be above and you will not be
beneath, if you listen to the commandments of
the LORD your God, which I am commanding
you today, to observe and to do them.*

—**DEUTERONOMY 28:13**

THIS HEADSHIP DECLARATION was initially spoken to
the nation of Israel. At the beginning of the Israelites' entrance into the land of promise, God wanted
certain important truths to be established in their minds.
By divine direction six tribes stood on the slopes of Mount
Ebal to shout amen to the curses of the Law. About five
hundred yards away the other six tribes stood on the slopes
of Mount Gerizim to shout amen to the blessings of the
Law. (See Deuteronomy 27:12–28:68.) A special altar was
erected in the valley between the mountains, and from that
area the Levites declared the word of the Lord, including
the proclamation of headship above.

Of all the nations of the world, why did God choose
Israel for such a high calling? Deuteronomy 7:7–8 explains
the answer:

> The LORD did not set His love on you nor choose you
> because you were more in number than any of the

peoples, for you were the fewest of all the peoples. But it is because the LORD loved you and because He kept the oath which He swore to your fathers.

Here we see evidence of the mustard seed principle, a fundamental characteristic of the kingdom of God. Just as the mustard seed is the "least of all seeds" but becomes "the greatest among herbs," so the Creator often chooses people and things considered the lowest, the last, and the least. Then He transforms them into the highest, the first, and the greatest—to reveal His power and give glory to His name (Matt. 13:31–32, MKJV; see Rom. 9:17). Though God is not confined to this pattern, He often moves this way.

God intended Israel to be the head in every arena of human experience: politically, militarily, socially, scientifically, educationally, monetarily, materially, religiously, and spiritually. In achieving excellence and preeminence, they were to become the exemplary nation—a living testimony of what can happen when an entire nation walks in covenant with God.

For a season it worked mightily, but then everything fell apart, and the Israelites became slaves to five successive Gentile empires—the Assyrians, the Babylonians, the Persians, the Grecians, and finally the Romans. For centuries instead of being "the head," they became "the tail," just as God forewarned (Deut. 28:43–44). A single two-letter word was the main stumbling block—the word *if*.

God promised to exalt them to the highest place only *if* they obeyed the Torah (Genesis through Deuteronomy). Under the old covenant especially, headship depended mostly on human performance, the ability of the Israelite people to flawlessly abide by the Law. The final curse declared by the Levites surely must have caused their hearts to tremble.

> "Cursed is he who does not confirm all the words of this law by doing them." And all the people shall say, "Amen."
> —Deuteronomy 27:26

From the moment they shouted amen, the heavy responsibility of keeping all 613 commandments of the Torah loomed over them. As failures and disobedience increased, over a period of centuries, the situation grew increasingly hopeless. It looked as if God's promises would fail.

But then Jesus came.

The mustard seed principle was evidenced marvelously in the incarnation of the Son of God. His birthplace, Bethlehem, was the least of all the cities of Judah, and He—the Creator of the universe—was born in the most unlikely accommodations in that city—a stable. After thirty-three years He was crucified and sunk to an even lower place of degradation, bearing "our sins in His own body on the tree" (1 Pet. 2:24). On the cross He absorbed all the vileness of humanity, becoming the vilest of all. He who was rightfully the head of all things became the tail by identifying with us in our fallen state. But not for long. Three days later He "redeemed us from the curse of the law" when He rose from the grave (Gal. 3:13).

The next passage speaks of the resurrection and ascension, when the Father's mighty power was released.

Which He performed in Christ when He raised Him from the dead and seated Him at His own right hand in the heavenly places, far above all principalities, and power, and might, and dominion, and every name that is named, not only in this age but also in that which is to come. And *He put all things in subjection under His feet and made Him the head over all things for the church*, which is His body, the fullness of Him who fills all things in all ways.

—EPHESIANS 1:20–23, EMPHASIS ADDED

The Amplified Bible, Classic Edition adds that this is "a headship exercised throughout the church."

Jesus came down to our level to lift us up to His level. Through the blood that cleanses us, the Spirit that enlivens us, the name that delivers us, and the covenant that empowers us, we are exalted over every enemy: sin, Satan, self, death, the grave, and eternal destruction.

Since Jesus is the head and we are His body, if all things are "under His feet," all things are under our feet as well. Even personal failures—if yielded to God—become stepping-stones instead of stumbling stones. Instead of portals leading to death, they become gateways of redemption leading to life—the life-giving principles that rule the kingdom of light. That's why God describes our status as being "above" only.

At the end of this age this promise will be fulfilled in greater ways than ever before. Both the true church and the nation of Israel will be increasingly scorned by the world. At the climax all nations will gather together against

Jerusalem in that infamous battle called Armageddon. Yet right at the critical moment, when destruction seems inevitable, Jesus will descend in all His glory. He will set up His throne in Jerusalem. Then the "Israel of God," composed of all who have ever walked in covenant with God (old and new), will be the governmental head of all nations and, ultimately, the head of the new creation (Gal. 6:16).

God did not say, "I will give you the potential of being the head"; He said, "I will make you the head and not the tail." This is something God is in the process of doing. It is His grace, wisdom, and power, not our human effort, that will cause this awesome reality to manifest on an ultimate level. If this is true in an eternal sense, shouldn't we manifest headship in lesser ways during our earthly sojourn?

ARRESTED IN ATLANTA

One of the greatest examples I could give of this truth concerns the night I spent in the Atlanta jail—yes, you read that correctly, but it didn't happen because I committed a crime. Let me explain.

I was conducting a tent meeting in northern Atlanta, just off I-75. Every night after church I took a team of young people down to Peachtree Street in downtown Atlanta to witness. It was one of the worst areas of Atlanta, rife with drug trafficking, prostitution, drunkenness, and perversity—the very type of people Jesus commissioned us to reach. That night, though, it backfired—or seemed to—but the sovereign God was on the throne, in control of every detail, and in amazing ways He determined to lift us above the negative circumstance to a place of power, purpose, and influence.

About six of us were sharing the gospel with different individuals when I heard a woman angrily screaming at a young Canadian in my youth group. She was a taxicab driver—rough looking and very masculine in her appearance and mannerisms. My youth group member had peacefully approached her and handed her a tract, saying, "Jesus loves you!" She immediately flew into a tirade filled with expletives: "I don't want your *** tract! I don't need your *** God! Now, get out of my *** way!"

Pressing her gas pedal to the floor and squealing her tires, she attempted to run him over. Extremely concerned, I ran across the street to see if I could help defuse the situation. Before I had a chance to get involved, she whipped her car around and sped out of sight. We found out afterward that she drove half a mile away and told a police officer the young man had assaulted her.

It was quite a surprise when a police car (blue lights flashing and siren blaring) pulled into a driveway about thirty feet away. The officer jumped out, ran over to the young man, twisted his arm behind his back, and began pulling him toward the police car. I rushed over and attempted to respectfully intervene, but the policeman cut me off, cursing at me and saying, "Get out of my way, you ***! I don't have time for you." I protested, "But officer, I'm in charge of a Christian youth group in the area tonight. We're just sharing the gospel. He's done nothing wrong."

The officer responded angrily again, pulling my youth group member forcefully toward his vehicle.

Finally reaching his car, he shoved the boy in the back seat and slammed the door shut. Exasperated at the injustice of it all, I shouted, "Are you going to tell us what you're charging him with?" His response was a blank stare.

"Are you going to tell us where you're taking him?" Still no answer, just a hostile glare.

Reaching the limits of my patience, I insisted, "OK, I'm responsible for this young man. He's a guest from another country. So where he goes, I go!" With that statement I opened the back door to the police car and sat inside (putting myself under arrest—which was technically illegal, but the next day the judge told me she didn't blame me for doing it). Right before I closed the door, I urged my wife, Elizabeth (who was the assistant youth director at that time): "Call every newspaper and every radio station and TV station in town, and tell them how unjustly we are being treated."

The officer was very obliging. He called for a paddy wagon, and they hauled us off. For the first hour after they booked us, we were in different cells. Then they brought the young man into my cell. I slapped him on the back and said, "Sing, Silas, sing!" So at two o'clock in the morning we began singing, praying, and preaching—loud enough that all the prisoners around us and on the floor above us could hear. (We were a little disappointed that God did not send an earthquake as He did for Paul.)

Meanwhile, Elizabeth had secured enough money to bail us out of jail at about 3:30 a.m. The next day we appeared before a judge. I opted to defend myself instead of using a court-appointed lawyer. The courtroom was full of believers who came to intercede. While sharing my story, I mentioned that the officer had admitted to us the night before, as we were waiting for the paddy wagon, that he had been watching us for several nights and knew what we were doing. When I divulged that information, he flew into a rage, cursing and screaming at us right in the courtroom. Two fellow officers had to drag him out. That turned everything in our favor. The case was thrown out of court. We were both set free and back at the tent that night for the service.

Meanwhile one radio station in town carried the story of a Pentecostal-Charismatic tent minister who had spent much of the night in an Atlanta jail on what appeared to be false charges. A pimp happened to be listening to the broadcast and commented to one of his prostitutes, "I could relate to that preacher; I've spent many nights in that jail." They came and parked outside to listen. About halfway through my message Elizabeth felt a strong compulsion to go out into the parking lot, and she saw them sitting there. As she began witnessing, the young girl broke down crying, confessing that she was a backslider. Her pimp got extremely nervous (apparently thinking he might lose control of her), so he cranked up his pickup truck and left as quick as possible.

The next day, she got word to Elizabeth that she was desperate to change her life. She confided that the prostitution ring ran a restaurant close by our tent where all the hookers worked as waitresses during the day and then walked the streets at night. (Apparently they laundered their money through the restaurant.) She begged Elizabeth to pull up behind the restaurant at exactly two o'clock in the afternoon. Her plan was to run out, jump in the car, and escape that self-destructive lifestyle. Elizabeth boldly agreed. When she pulled up, the young girl bolted out the back door and jumped into the car, and they sped off to the tent where we were already conducting an afternoon service that Sunday.

When they arrived, she threw the car door open, jumped out, and ran to the altar. We stopped everything to pray with her. She sobbed in repentance for a long time; then she looked up anxiously and said, "If he finds me, he'll kill me. I have to leave Atlanta."

I said, "Where are you from?"

She mentioned a certain city in North Carolina. A lady who was at the altar praying for her stopped and looked up at her, wide-eyed; she lived just a few miles away from that community. Excitedly she explained how God had awakened her that morning and told her to drive to Atlanta for the service that day. She had to leave immediately after church to get back in time for work the next morning. With a broad smile on my face, I pointed to the woman's car in the parking lot and said to God's prodigal daughter, "Your chauffeur-driven limousine awaits." (Isn't that just like our loving heavenly Father?) Thinking the pimp might show up at any moment, they rushed away.

He did show up—within the hour—quite angry and evidently drunk or high. Waving a gun around threateningly, he yelled, "I know she must have come here. I know you took her somewhere. If you don't tell me where she is, I'll kill all of you." He kept ranting and raving, but we continued calmly and lovingly sharing the gospel. For two more days he kept returning, trying to intimidate us. He even drove his car into the side of the tent and snapped a couple of ropes. We kept praying and believing. Finally, around the fourth day, he got out of his truck and walked up to the tent, weeping and begging us to pray with him. That day he gave his heart to the Lord.

Then he pleaded with us for the girl's phone number. "We can't do that," we responded. "We promised to keep her location a secret."

He kept at it, attending the meetings at night and pleading with us. Finally we called and asked how she felt about it. She agreed to let him call her on the phone. When they talked, she agreed to let him drive up and visit her. During that visit—are you ready for this—he asked her to marry him. And yes, she agreed—but only if they lived a Christian life together (which they did). Out of the pit of depravity into a place of purity and peace—that's about how drastic the change was in both of their lives.

That's how the headship promise manifested for us that notable night. The hostility of the taxicab driver, the false arrest, the temporary incarceration, the news report—that was all the enemy's attempt to push us to the bottom. But God sovereignly seized the situation and made it fulfill His purpose, lifting us from the bottom to the top, making us "the head and not the tail" (Deut. 28:13).

Two related promises helped usher us into victory that night:

1. When the enemy comes in like a flood, the Spirit of the LORD will lift up a standard against him (Isa. 59:19).

2. He "always causes us to triumph in Christ" (2 Cor. 2:14).

Start claiming these yourself! Then expect God to lift you miraculously from the bottom to the top.

POWERFUL PROCLAMATION

I proclaim that I am the head and not the tail; I always live above and never beneath. Even in trials, tribulations, persecutions, and failures, I am triumphant, for nothing can separate me from the love of God. No weapon formed against me shall prosper. All things will work together for my good. Because all things are under Jesus's feet, all things are under my feet. Because Jesus has ascended far above all things, in Him I have ascended far above all things. In the kingdom to come, I will rule and reign with Him in a restored paradise world that He will establish when He returns. *These are God's promises to me. I claim these supernatural impartations and expect their manifestation in my life.*

Additional Insights: Psalm 27:6;
Ephesians 4:15; Colossians 2:10, 18–19

METAMORPHOSIS

*But we all, seeing the glory of the Lord with
unveiled faces, as in a mirror, are being
transformed into the same image from glory
to glory by the Spirit of the Lord.*

—2 CORINTHIANS 3:18

THE WORD TRANSFORMED in this scripture is from the Greek word *metamorphoo* (pronounced *met-am-or-fo'-o*), from which we get our English word *metamorphosis* (meaning a complete change in appearance, character, or circumstance). I am very familiar with this interesting term. As a boy, I collected caterpillars, stored them in an aquarium, watched them weave their cocoons, and then taped those cocoons to the walls of my bedroom. Weeks and months later I enjoyed the amazing spectacle of butterflies emerging, flying all around the room, and perching on my fingers or nose. It never got old; it was so inspiring to my young mind. Metamorphosis! What a power word! And how this process of nature speaks of far-more-powerful supernatural realities!

Metamorphoo is only found four times in the New Testament. Two of those times it is translated into the word *transfigured*—when it described what happened to Jesus on the holy mountain where He was transformed into a radiant being and appeared with Moses and Elijah to the three chief disciples, Peter, James, and John. It was a wonderful foreshadowing of what is going to happen for all of us in the kingdom which is yet to come.

Right now, however, the metamorphosis is in the "cocoon" stage: internal, invisible, and spiritual. Every day those who are yielded to God are being transformed into the character of the Lord Jesus from glory to glory—emerging from every trial and challenge with more of His love, joy, peace, righteousness, and all His other attributes. According to our foundation scripture, God uses two main spiritual influences to accomplish this goal:

+ **The Word of God:** We see the glory of the Lord "as in a mirror." The mirror is the Word of God. In its wonderful stories and teachings, the character of the unseen God is clearly seen. (See James 1:23–24.) As we gaze on this reflection of "the glory of the Lord," we are "transformed into the same image," taking on the Lord's attributes (2 Cor. 3:18).

+ **The Spirit of God:** This transformation is accomplished by "the Spirit of the Lord," the power of the Highest that dwells within our hearts (v. 18).

One primary way these two influences bring forth supernatural transformation in us is by using the circumstances of life, both good and bad. The promises of Romans 8:28–29 are so encouraging:

We know that all things work together for good to those who love God, to those who are called according to His purpose. For those whom He foreknew, He predestined to be conformed to the image of His Son, so that He might be the firstborn among many brothers.

What a blessing! No matter what we face in life—the good and the bad—it's all going to carry us closer to this goal of transformation. God doesn't author the bad things, but He is a genius at using them to promote His purpose.

God's original purpose ("Let us make man in our image," found in Genesis 1:26) is still an ongoing process. Though man fell into a spiritual abyss, God never changed His agenda. Even when we face negatives, God turns them into positives.

- When we experience hurt from others, God uses that to develop the divine trait of forgiveness in us.

- When we witness the suffering of others, God awakens the divine trait of compassion in us.

- When we go through personal failure, God pours out His mercy on us and makes us more merciful toward others in the process.

The forgiving, compassionate, and merciful Savior is transforming us into forgiving, compassionate, and merciful offspring. The image is being transferred. To embrace the process, we need to think God thoughts and see things from God's perspective. For this reason we are commanded:

Do not be conformed to this world, but be transformed [Gr. *metamorphoo*] by the renewing of your mind, that you may prove what is the good and acceptable and perfect will of God.

—Romans 12:2

Thankfully the cocoon stage will soon be over, and the butterflies will emerge. The divine plan will reach its zenith at the coming of the Lord, when the dead will rise and, along with living believers, be caught up to meet Him in the air.

Beloved, now are we children of God, and it has not yet been revealed what we shall be. But we know that when He appears, we shall be like Him, for we shall see Him as He is.

—1 John 3:2

For this corruptible will put on incorruption, and this mortal will put on immortality. When this corruptible will have put on incorruption, and this mortal will have put on immortality, then the saying that is written shall come to pass: "Death is swallowed up in victory."

—1 Corinthians 15:53–54

These two passages are just cracking the door open on the glorious future God has in store for His people. We will throw that door wide open in the next two chapters.

POWERFUL PROCLAMATION

I proclaim that I am involved in a process of transformation that will cause me to pass from glory to glory. In this life I will experience the glory of being conformed to the nature of the Lord Jesus internally on my way to the ultimate experience of being changed into His likeness externally and completely when He returns. God will cause every negative thing I face in life to work toward this final goal. *This is God's promise to me. I claim this supernatural impartation and expect its manifestation in my life.*

Additional Insights: Isaiah 26:19; Romans 8:30; 2 Corinthians 4:15–18; Philippians 3:20–21

MANSIONS IN HEAVEN—OR SOMETHING FAR GREATER?

Let not your heart be troubled; you believe in God, believe also in Me. In My Father's house are many mansions; if it were not so, I would have told you. I go to prepare a place for you.

—JOHN 14:1–2, NKJV

I N THE LATTER part of His earthly ministry Jesus encouraged His followers with this often-quoted and much-loved promise. Soon after voicing this promise, He was crucified, resurrected, and ascended into heaven. Apparently He wanted to assure His disciples before He left that their future was secure. He was planning for their eventual transition into a heavenly realm as well. Both the King James Version and the New King James Version use the word *mansions* in prophetically describing our ultimate destination. But are large, luxurious homes what Jesus had in mind when He gave this pledge?

There are four main reasons we live in homes in this physical world: first, so families can dwell together; second, to protect us from the elements; third, to provide a safe, enclosed place for eating and sleeping; and fourth, to store our possessions. Quite likely none of these things will be necessary for glorified saints who will shine like "the sun" in the kingdom of God (Matt. 13:43).

Notice Jesus said these mansions are located in the "Father's house." Ponder that wording for a moment. Dare to ask yourself questions such as, "Where is God's house?" and "How big is God's house?" Isaiah 66:1 alludes to possible answers: "Heaven is My throne, and the earth is My footstool. Where then is the house that you could build for Me? And where is the place of My rest?"

A throne and a footstool are just two small pieces of furniture in a house that is far bigger. The "Father's house" must be larger than both natural and spiritual universes, just as incalculable in size as the Creator Himself. Isaiah 57:15 bluntly states that God "inhabits eternity."

If the "Father's house" is that huge, what did Jesus mean by "mansions"? Look at the original Greek. The word translated "mansions" is *mone* (pronounced *mo-nay'*), only found twice in the New Testament, both times in John chapter 14 (verses 2 and 23). Here is the Amplified Bible, Classic Edition of the second occurrence:

> Jesus answered, If a person [really] loves Me, he will keep My word [obey My teaching]; and My Father will love him, and We will come to him and make *Our home (abode, special dwelling place)* with him.
>
> —JOHN 14:23, AMPC, EMPHASIS ADDED

In this verse *mone* is translated home, abode, and special dwelling place.

If we apply this to John 14:2, we could interpret the Son of God's words as meaning, "In My Father's house are many special dwelling places, many abodes or spheres of existence." If you stretch that out to encompass both the physical and the spiritual universes, the possibilities are beyond our ability to imagine.

How do you wrap your mind around the immensity of that pledge? The best response may be 1 Corinthians 2:9: "Eye has not seen, nor ear heard, nor has it entered into the heart of man the things which God has prepared for those who love Him."

What is the place Jesus is preparing for His own? I suppose it could be palatial houses on celestial hillsides—but by now I think you agree, it's probably something far more glorious.

POWERFUL PROCLAMATION

I proclaim that God is preparing a special dwelling place for me in the eternal expanses of the celestial world. Though this future paradise is beyond my ability to comprehend, I know it will be spectacular—above and beyond anything I could ask or think. In that day, along with the rest of the body of Christ, I will experience "fullness of joy" in the presence of the King of all kings and at His right hand "pleasures for evermore" (Ps. 16:11). *This is God's promise to me. I claim this supernatural impartation and expect its manifestation in my life.*

Additional Insights: Jeremiah 29:11;
John 16:13–15; Romans 8:32; Revelation 3:12

THE FINAL PROMISE

He who testifies to these things says, "Surely I am coming soon." Amen. Even so, come Lord Jesus!
—**REVELATION 22:20**

T HE VERSE ABOVE comes right before the closing verse of the Book of Revelation. It is the Bible's last promise—the King of kings declaring His soon return. This spectacular pledge is closer to fulfillment than ever. Skeptics are quick to point out that for centuries Christians have heralded Jesus's return, yet it still has not taken place. However, "The Lord is not slack concerning His promise, as some count slackness, but is longsuffering toward us, not willing that any should perish but that all should come to repentance" (2 Pet. 3:9, NKJV).

Some of the most powerful Old Testament promises pointed to the first coming of the Messiah (when He became as we are). Some of the most powerful New Testament promises point to His second coming (when we will become as He is). Various prophetic pledges, old and new, reveal unique features of this glorious event.

+ Jesus will "descend from heaven with a shout, with the voice of the archangel, and with the trumpet call of God" (1 Thess. 4:16).

+ He will appear in "flaming fire," with "all the holy
  angels" (2 Thess. 1:8; Matt. 25:31).

+ During that pivotal event, "the light of the moon
  shall be as the light of the sun, and the light of
  the sun shall be sevenfold, as the light of seven
  days" (Isa. 30:26).

+ The "veil" of flesh-consciousness "spread over all
  nations" will be destroyed (Isa. 25:7).

+ Those who are "dead in Christ" will be resurrected
  and glorified first. Then all living believers will
  be caught up "to meet the Lord in the air," to be
  changed "in a moment, in the twinkling of an eye"
  (1 Thess. 4:16–17; see also 1 Cor. 15:50–57). We
  will then return with Him to occupy this world.

+ When the Son of God descends, "His feet will
  stand on the Mount of Olives," and it will "split
  in two halves by a very great valley" (Zech. 14:4).

+ The Antichrist (the "lawless one") will be
  destroyed by "the brightness of His presence"
  (2 Thess. 2:8).

+ "The kings of the earth with their armies" will be
  conquered (Rev. 19:19).

+ "The kingdom and dominion, and the greatness of
  all the kingdoms under the whole heaven, shall
  be given to the people of the saints of the Most
  High" (Dan. 7:27).

+ "The meek" will "inherit the earth," and we will
  finally "see His face"" (Matt. 5:5; Rev. 22:4).

- "Living water will flow out from Jerusalem," bringing divine life to everything and everyone in the world (Zech. 14:8).

- The Messiah "shall judge among the nations, and shall rebuke many peoples; and they shall beat their swords into plowshares, and their spears into pruning hooks; nation shall not lift up sword against nation, nor shall they learn war any more" (Isa. 2:4).

- Such heavenly love and peace will envelop the earth that "the wolf and the lamb shall feed together, and the lion shall eat straw like the bull.... They shall not hurt nor destroy in all My holy mountain, says the LORD" (Isa. 65:25).

- Jerusalem will become the world's capital, and the government of God will be established globally. The redeemed of the Lord will be "kings and priests unto our God; and we shall reign on the earth" (Rev. 5:10; see also Isa. 9:6–7).

- Satan will be bound in "a bottomless pit" (Rev. 20:1–3).

These are all powerful descriptions of events coinciding with His second coming, but what will Jesus miraculously perform in us when we see Him? The following points will fill your heart with awe.

TEN WAYS WE WILL BE "LIKE HIM"

When Jesus makes His magnificent entrance into this world, He will transform "our body of humiliation, so that it may be conformed to His glorious body" (Phil. 3:21). In one stroke of artistic genius the heavenly potter will fashion us "like Him" in ten primary ways (1 John 3:2):

1. We will be like Him in appearance (Rev. 1:16; Matt. 13:43).

2. We will be like Him in authority (Ps. 8:4–6; Rev. 3:21).

3. We will be like Him in intelligence (John 15:15; 1 Cor. 13:12).

4. We will be like Him in emotions (John 14:27; 15:11; 17:26).

5. We will be like Him in supernatural abilities (John 14:12).

6. We will be like Him in oneness with the Father (John 17:20–21).

7. We will be like Him in glory (John 17:22).

8. We will be like Him in holiness (1 Pet. 1:16; Eph. 1:4; Rev. 22:11).

9. We will be like Him in perfection (John 17:23; Col. 1:28).

10. We will be like Him in unchangeableness (Mal. 3:6; Rev. 3:12).

Two of the most intriguing promises concerning our future state are:

+ **The impartation of divine knowledge:** "For now we see as through a glass, dimly, but then, face to face. Now I know in part, but then I shall know, *even as I also am known*" (1 Cor. 13:12, emphasis added). In other words, our knowledge of God will be as complete as His knowledge of us.

+ **The expression of God's fullness:** "When all things are subjected to Him, then the Son Himself will also be subject to Him who put all things under Him, *that God may be all in all*" (1 Cor. 15:28, emphasis added; see also John 1:16). In other words, God will express Himself fully in each one of His offspring.

No wonder the "whole creation groans and travails in pain together until now" (like a mother in labor) waiting for the full "manifestation of the sons of God" (Rom. 8:19, 22, KJV).

> Because the creation itself also will be delivered from the bondage of corruption into the glorious liberty of the children of God.
> —ROMANS 8:21, NKJV

You see, we are the "firstfruits" of a transformational process that will ultimately seize the whole cosmos. This metamorphosis began invisibly and internally in the hearts of the children of promise; it will end visibly and externally, pervading the entire universe.

> The heavens will be dissolved, being on fire, and the elements will melt with fervent heat....Nevertheless we,

according to His promise, look for new heavens and a new
earth in which righteousness dwells.

—2 PETER 3:12–13, NKJV, EMPHASIS ADDED

What a glorious era that will be!

FIFTEEN PROMISES GIVEN TO OVERCOMERS

As we enter this coming age of perfection, Jesus will
confer heavenly benefits on His people without delay. He
announced in the last chapter of the Book of the Revelation:

I am coming quickly, and My reward is with Me, to give
to every one according to his work.

—REVELATION 22:12, NKJV

Though this final book of the Bible forecasts very tumul-
tuous times soon, it also unveils fifteen ultimate promises
given to the overcomers—those who "overcome" the temp-
tations, deceptions, satanic wiles, and curses that abound
in this valley of the shadow of death. I urge you to read
these passages worshipfully with a heart full of joyous
anticipation:

To him who overcomes I will give to eat from the tree of
life, which is in the midst of the Paradise of God.

—REVELATION 2:7, NKJV

Be faithful unto death, and I will give you the crown
of life.

—REVELATION 2:10

He who overcomes shall not be hurt by the second death.

—REVELATION 2:11

To him who overcomes I will give the hidden manna to eat.

—REVELATION 2:17

And I will give him a white stone, and on the stone a new name written, which no one knows except he who receives it.

—REVELATION 2:17

To him who overcomes and keeps My works to the end, I will give authority over the nations—He "shall rule them with a rod of iron; like the vessels of a potter they shall be broken in pieces"—even as I myself have received authority from My Father.

—REVELATION 2:26–27

And I will give him the morning star.

—REVELATION 2:28

He who overcomes shall be clothed in white garments.

—REVELATION 3:5

I will not blot his name out of the Book of Life.

—REVELATION 3:5

I will confess his name before My Father and before His angels.

—REVELATION 3:5

He who overcomes will I make a pillar in the temple of My God, and he shall go out no more.

—REVELATION 3:12

I will write on him the name of My God and the name of the city of My God, the New Jerusalem, which comes down out of heaven from My God, and My own new name.

—REVELATION 3:12

To him who overcomes will I grant to sit with Me on My throne, as I also overcame and sat down with My Father on His throne.

—REVELATION 3:21

He who overcomes shall inherit all things.

—REVELATION 21:7

…and I will be his God and he shall be My son.

—REVELATION 21:7

At this point you must feel like dropping to your knees with an overwhelming sense of gratitude or leaping to your feet with an ecstatic shout of praise. Words such as *amazing, remarkable, astounding,* and *phenomenal* are too weak to describe such an indescribable future—something we could never earn by our own efforts.

However, if God could supernaturally move the wooden church in Swan Quarter, North Carolina, to the plot of ground where He wanted it (if you read chapter 3, you understand), then He can supernaturally move the church of the living God to this spectacular future position in His everlasting kingdom—ultimately to dwell forevermore in that celestial "city which has foundations, whose builder and maker is God" (Heb. 11:10).

The beloved apostle who received this list of fifteen promises in the Book of Revelation summed it up in one simple sentence in his first epistle: "This is the promise that He has promised us—eternal life" (1 John 2:25).

Yes, of all the 7,487 promises, "this is *the* promise."

POWERFUL PROCLAMATION

I proclaim that Jesus is returning and that I will be rewarded for serving Him. He has promised that I will eat of the tree of life (God's nature) and of hidden manna (the deeper revelation of His mysteries). I will be clothed in white garments (covered with God's righteousness). My name will remain forever in the Book of Life. As a glorified king/priest, I will be a pillar in the temple of God (ruling and reigning with Christ over the new creation), and I will share the throne (the authority and dominion) of the almighty God. Along with the rest of the body of Christ, I will inherit all things and live eternally in a glorified, celestial state. *These are God's promises to me. I claim these supernatural impartations and expect these manifestations in my life.*

Additional Insights: Romans 8:18–25;
Ephesians 5:27; 1 Corinthians 15:50–58; Revelation 20–22

Conclusion

PRAYING THE PROMISES

T HESE PROMISES ARE a part of you now.
As Kenneth Hagin once said, "You are what you read."[1] So these promises are not just concepts you have stored on the dusty shelves of your mind; they are manna from heaven you have digested into your regenerated spirit. They are a part of your sonship identity now, a substantial aspect of who you are in Christ.

Like the mysterious hormone called adrenaline, these promises will abide within you, secretly, peacefully, and patiently, waiting for that moment when life pressures you beyond your capacity to sufficiently respond—then they will rush with Godspeed to the affected area, granting you supernatural strength, not only to endure but to overcome.

Brother Hagin also insisted, "Prayer is successful only when it is based on the promises in God's Word."[2] After you close this book, make a strong determination that from now on you're going to quit praying problems and start praying promises. No longer will you spend precious hours of intercession reminding God of the conflicts, the disappointments, the failures, the hindrances, the battles, and the challenges; instead, you intend to remind Him of the commitments He has made to you in His Word.

When the children of Israel had been in Egyptian bondage over four centuries, Scripture states that they "sighed because of the bondage, and they cried" and "God heard their groaning," but that was not the reason God moved so powerfully on their behalf (Exod. 2:23–24). At the same time, there were probably millions of other enslaved and oppressed people in the world sighing, crying, and groaning—yet the Creator did not respond to them with such a supernatural display of power. What made the difference? The last part of verse 24 reveals the secret: "God remembered His covenant." That's why He treated the Israelites differently.

But you have "a better covenant…established on better promises" (Heb. 8:6, a scripture I already emphasized in one of the opening chapters). How much more should you expect divine intervention!

One of my favorite verses in the Bible contains four promises I want to share with you at the close of this book: "Those who wait upon the Lord shall renew their strength; they shall mount up with wings as eagles, they shall run and not be weary, and they shall walk and not faint" (Isa. 40:31).

As a final prayerful act of worship, based on all that you have read so far, claim that beautiful fourfold pledge right now. Spend some time waiting on the Lord, claiming the promises dearest to your heart, and then start soaring on the wings of hope and peace.

+ *Mount up* above the clouds where the sun always shines, then…

+ *Run* with the vision God has given you and *walk* in the light, dispelling darkness everywhere you go.

+ Your *strength has been renewed* by the One who said, "If you ask anything in My name, I will do it" (John 14:14).

There are so many promises we haven't spotlighted yet—thousands of pledges I would like to share with you that cover every area of need in our lives—but we have run out of space.

Twenty-five primary promises have been emphasized so far, with two hundred seventy-five other promises used in explanations (three hundred total). That's enough to win any battle. All Gideon needed was three hundred men to blow shofars, break lamps, and shine their lights to scatter the Midianite army. All you need to emerge triumphant on your personal battlefield are the three hundred divine pledges we have celebrated. Now, like one of Gideon's soldiers, lift your voice like a shofar! Proclaim these promises with audacious faith! Don't hide them in your heart! Break the lamp of the Word open and shine the light of truth!

Now, stand your ground and watch the enemy scatter!

The time for victory has come.

LIST OF PROMISES

T HOUGH TWENTY-FIVE PRIMARY promises have been emphasized in this book, a total of three hundred promises are referenced. So that you will have a complete overview of all the promises from God included, the following list is provided. This list does not include any other promises that might be found in those passages listed in the "Additional Insights" feature.

SECTION I
ESTABLISHING THE REVELATION

1. All the promises of God in Christ are yes and amen (2 Cor. 1:20).

CHAPTER 1
PROMISES, PROMISES—
AND ALL OF THEM TRUE!

2. "The joy of the LORD is [our] strength" (Neh. 8:10).

3. God "gives power to the faint" (Isa. 40:29).

4. God increases the strength of those who are weak (Isa. 40:29).

5. Jesus authors our faith (Heb. 12:2).

6. Jesus will finish our faith (Heb. 12:2).

7. "The prayer of faith [saves] the sick" (James 5:15).

8. God raises up the sick (James 5:15).

9. God gives His people power to get wealth (Deut. 8:18).

10. God will never leave His people (Heb. 13:5).

11. God will never forsake His people (Heb. 13:5).

12. Believers will be resurrected (John 11:25).

CHAPTER 2
THE MYSTERY OF THE RAINBOW

13. God promised to establish a covenant with Noah (Gen. 9:9).

14. God promised that the rainbow would be seen in a cloud when it rains (Gen. 9:13–14).

15. God promised that the rainbow would be a sign of His covenant (Gen. 9:13–14).

16. God promised to remember His covenant with Noah (Gen. 9:15).

17. God promised to never send a global flood again (Gen. 9:15).

CHAPTER 3
PATRIARCH OF THE PROMISES

18. Abraham's seed would be like the dust (Gen. 13:16).

19. Abraham's seed would be like the stars (Gen. 22:17).

20. Abraham's seed would be like the sand (Gen. 22:17).

21. Abraham would be blessed (Gen. 12:2).

22. Abraham's name would be made great (Gen. 12:2).

23. Abraham would be made a blessing (Gen. 12:3).

24. Through Abraham and his descendants, "all families of the earth [would] be blessed" (Gen. 12:3).

25. Through Abraham and his descendants, "all the nations of the earth [would] be blessed" (Gen. 26:4).

26. Abraham's seed would spend four centuries in bondage but "will come out with great possessions" (Gen. 15:14).

27. Abraham's seed would "possess the gate of their enemies" (Gen. 22:17).

28. The gates of Hades (death) will not prevail against the church (Matt. 16:18; this verse and promise are also mentioned in promise 1, the chapter on "Divine Revelation," but not listed there).

CHAPTER 4
NOT ONE WORD WILL FAIL

29. All necessary material things will be added to those who seek the kingdom of God first (Matt. 6:33).

30. Our times are in God's hands (Ps. 31:15).

31. Those who mourn (grieved and repentant over sin) will be blessed (Matt. 5:4).

32. Those who mourn (grieved and repentant over sin) will be comforted by God (Matt. 5:4).

33. The merciful will be blessed (Matt. 5:7).

34. The merciful will obtain mercy (Matt. 5:7).

35. The pure in heart will be blessed (Matt. 5:8).

36. The pure in heart will see God (Matt. 5:8).

37. We are healed by the stripes of Jesus (Isa. 53:5).

38. "To be absent from the body [is] to be present with the Lord" (2 Cor. 5:8).

Chapter 5
Receiving a New Identity

39. The helper (the Holy Spirit) would come after Jesus's departure (John 16:7, NKJV).

40. The helper would "convict the world of sin" (John 16:8, NKJV).

41. The helper would "convict the world of… righteousness" (John 16:8, NKJV).

42. The helper would "convict the world of… judgment" (John 16:8, NKJV).

43. "The goodness of God leads [us] to repentance" (Rom. 2:4).

44. Those who seek God with all their heart and soul find Him (Deut. 4:29).

45. "Ask and it will be given to you" (Matt. 7:7).

46. "Seek and you will find" (Matt. 7:7).

47. "Knock and it will be opened to you" (Matt. 7:7).

48. Whoever calls on the Lord's name will be saved (Acts 2:21; the original promise from Joel 2:32 is quoted in promise 20 but not listed there).

49. Those who confess Jesus as Lord and believe in their hearts God has raised Him from the dead are saved (Rom. 10:9).

50. Those who repent and convert experience the wiping away of sins (Acts 3:19).

51. Those who repent and convert experience "times of refreshing…from the presence of the Lord" (Acts 3:19).

52. Those who receive Jesus become children of God (John 1:12–13, NKJV).

53. Christ dwells in our hearts by faith (Eph. 3:17).

54. Those who believe in the Son have eternal life (John 3:36).

55. If anyone is in Christ, he or she is a new creation (2 Cor. 5:17).

56. If anyone is in Christ, "old things have passed away" (2 Cor. 5:17).

57. If anyone is in Christ, "all things have become new" (2 Cor. 5:17).

SECTION II
THE PROMISES

58. Those who receive God's promises "become partakers of the divine nature" (2 Pet. 1:4).

59. Those who receive God's promises "escape the corruption that is in the world through lust" (2 Pet. 1:4).

Promise 1
Divine Revelation

60. God's Spirit reveals the deep things of God to those who love Him (1 Cor. 2:10).

61. "It is given to [believers] to know the mysteries of the kingdom of heaven" (Matt. 13:11).

62. Good and perfect gifts come from above (James 1:17).

63. The church is built on the rock of divine revelation (Matt. 16:17–18).

64. The "breath of the Almighty" gives understanding to our spirits (Job 32:8).

65. The Holy Spirit was sent to guide us into all truth (John 16:13).

66. The "Spirit of wisdom and revelation" reveals the hope of our calling (Eph. 1:17–19).

67. The "Spirit of wisdom and revelation" reveals the riches of the glory of God's inheritance in us (Eph. 1:17–19).

68. The "Spirit of wisdom and revelation" reveals the greatness of God's power toward us (Eph. 1:17–19).

Promise 2
Inheriting God's Kingdom

69. God often chooses the poor to be "rich in faith" (James 2:5).

70. God gives His people faith as a gift (Eph. 2:8).

71. Those who partake of Jesus's death become prosperous (Ps. 22:29).

72. Kingdom citizens receive righteousness in the Holy Spirit (Rom. 14:17).

73. Kingdom citizens receive peace in the Holy Spirit (Rom. 14:17).

74. Kingdom citizens receive joy in the Holy Spirit (Rom. 14:17).

75. Kingdom citizens receive righteousness from God by faith (Phil. 3:9).

76. Believers experience peace that surpasses understanding (Phil. 4:7).

77. Believers know the love of God that surpasses knowledge (Eph. 3:19).

78. Believers are "filled with all the fullness of God" (Eph. 3:19).

79. The poor in spirit are blessed (Matt. 5:3).

80. The poor in spirit inherit the kingdom of heaven (Matt. 5:3).

81. Those who are born again are blessed to comprehend the kingdom of God (John 3:3).

82. Believers are delivered from the power of darkness (Col. 1:13).

83. Believers are transferred into the kingdom of God's Son (Col. 1:13).

84. The kingdom of God demonstrates itself with power in our lives (1 Cor. 4:20).

PROMISE 3
SHARING GOD'S THRONE

85. Dedicated believers are seated with God in His throne (Rev. 3:21).

86. Believers are made alive with Christ (Eph. 2:5).

87. Believers are raised up (resurrected) with Christ (Eph. 2:6).

88. Believers are seated "together in the heavenly places in Christ" (Eph. 2:6).

89. God raises the poor (in spirit) from the dust (1 Sam. 2:8).

90. God raises the oppressed from the dunghill (1 Sam. 2:8).

91. God's people are spiritually seated with princes (1 Sam. 2:8).

92. God's people "inherit a throne of glory" (1 Sam. 2:8).

93. When Jesus sent out His disciples, He "gave them power and authority over all demons and to cure diseases" (Luke 9:1). This is still His promise today.

94. God has promised in the last days that "the people who know their God shall be strong, and carry out great exploits" (Dan. 11:32, NKJV).

95. Because God's people share His throne, our enemies become our footstool (Mark 12:36, NKJV).

PROMISE 4
THE HUNDREDFOLD RETURN

96. Those who sacrifice certain aspects of earthly relationships for God's kingdom, in a healthy and proper way, receive a hundredfold (Mark 10:29–30).

97. Those who sacrifice possessions for God's kingdom receive a hundredfold (Mark 10:29–30).

98. Those who lose their lives for the sake of Jesus ultimately save their lives (Mark 8:35).

PROMISE 5
DIVINELY ORDERED STEPS

99. The steps of good people are ordered by the Lord (Ps. 37:23).

100. The wind of the Spirit will guide those who are born again into their future (John 3:8).

101. God will direct the paths of those who trust Him, lean not on their own understanding, and acknowledge Him in all their ways (Prov. 3:5–6).

PROMISE 6
THE POWER OF THE SPOKEN WORD

102. Our tongues have power over life and death (Prov. 18:21).

103. Those who love the revelation of the power of words "eat its fruit" (Prov. 18:21).

104. Those who abide in Christ ask what they desire, and it will be done (John 15:7, NKJV).

105. Those with mustard seed faith can uproot mulberry trees (Luke 17:6).

106. Believers who are strong in faith take the kingdom of God by force (Matt. 11:12).

PROMISE 7
BECOMING THE RIGHTEOUSNESS OF GOD

107. Believers "become the righteousness of God" in Christ (2 Cor. 5:21).

108. Jesus, "by the grace of God," experienced "death for everyone" (Heb. 2:9).

109. We receive grace and righteousness, and we reign in life through Jesus Christ (Rom. 5:17).

110. In the new covenant God places "a new spirit" in His people (Ezek. 36:26).

111. This "new man" is created "in true righteousness" (Eph. 4:24, NKJV).

112. With the heart God's people believe "unto righteousness" (Rom. 10:10).

113. In the new covenant God promises to give His people "beauty for ashes" (Isa. 61:3).

114. God fills "those who hunger and thirst for righteousness" (Matt. 5:6).

115. In God's sight believers are "holy and blameless" (Eph. 1:4).

PROMISE 8
CRUSHING SATAN

116. God will "crush Satan under [our] feet" (Rom. 16:20).

117. The seed of the woman was destined to crush the head of the serpent from the beginning (Gen. 3:14–15).

118. Believers in whom God's Word dwells have already overcome (1 John 2:14).

119. God's salvation will especially manifest in greatness of power when Satan is finally cast to the earth (Rev. 12:10).

120. God's strength will especially manifest when Satan is finally cast to the earth (Rev. 12:10).

121. God's kingdom will especially manifest when Satan is finally cast to the earth (Rev. 12:10).

122. The blood of Jesus makes us overcomers (Rev. 12:11).

123. Believers are "justified" by the blood of Jesus—legally acquitted of all guilt, just as if we never sinned (Rom. 5:9).

124. The word of our testimony, aligned with God's Word, makes us overcomers (Rev. 12:11).

125. Selflessness is necessary to be positioned in a place of overcoming power (Rev. 12:11).

126. God has given us authority "to trample on serpents and scorpions," symbolic of demonic powers (Luke 10:19).

127. God has given us authority "over all the power of the enemy" (Luke 10:19; this verse and promise are also used in promise 15 but not listed there).

128. Nothing will by any means hurt us (Luke 10:19).

129. Because we are of God, and because He who is in us is greater, we already have overcome the demonic powers rampant in this world (1 John 4:4; this verse and promise are also used in promise 15 but not listed there).

Promise 9
Exceedingly Abundantly Beyond

130. God "is able to do exceedingly abundantly beyond" anything we ask or think, according to the power that resides within us (Eph. 3:20).

Promise 10
Angelic Intervention

131. Angels are ministering spirits sent by God to minister to the heirs of salvation (Heb. 1:13–14).

132. God charges His angels to guard His people in all their ways (Ps. 91:11).

133. Angels are commanded to bear us up in their hands lest we dash our foot against a stone (Ps. 91:12).

134. Sometimes those who entertain strangers have "entertained angels unknowingly" (Heb. 13:2).

PROMISE 11
BLESSED WITH ALL SPIRITUAL BLESSINGS

135. God already "has blessed us with every spiritual blessing" (Eph. 1:3).

136. These blessings can be accessed in "the heavenly places in Christ" (Eph. 1:3).

137. Where two or three are gathered in the name of Jesus, He is in the midst (Matt. 18:20).

138. God has "led captivity captive"—He has already captivated anything that could potentially captivate His people (Ps. 68:18).

PROMISE 12
SPIRITUAL REVIVING

139. God promises to dwell in "the high and holy place" with those who have "a contrite and humble spirit" (Isa. 57:15).

140. God promises to revive those who have a contrite and humble spirit (Isa. 57:15).

141. God promises to lift up the humble (James 4:10).

142. God promises to exalt the humble (1 Pet. 5:6).

143. If you "believe in the Lord Jesus Christ…you and your household will be saved" (Acts 16:31).

144. God creates within His people "a new spirit" (Ezek. 11:19, similar to the promise of Ezek. 36:26, included in promise 20).

145. God removes from the repentant a "stony heart" of rebellion (Ezek. 11:19).

146. God gives the repentant "a heart of flesh," a heart that is sensitive and yielded (Ezek. 11:19).

PROMISE 13
GOD TURNS CURSES INTO BLESSINGS

147. "All things work together for good to those who love God, to those who are called according to His purpose" (Rom. 8:28).

PROMISE 14
INHABITING OUR PRAISE

148. God inhabits the praises of His people (Ps. 22:3).

PROMISE 15
SPIRITUAL WEAPONS

149. "The weapons of our warfare are not carnal, but mighty through God to the pulling down of strongholds" (2 Cor. 10:4).

150. "We have the mind of Christ" (1 Cor. 2:16).

151. "If God be for us, who can be against us?" (Rom. 8:31, KJV).

152. "There is therefore now no condemnation for those who are in Christ Jesus" (Rom. 8:1).

153. "The peace of God, which surpasses all understanding, will guard your hearts and minds through Christ Jesus" (Phil. 4:7, NKJV).

154. "For God has not given us a spirit of fear, but of power and of love and of a sound mind" (2 Tim. 1:7, NKJV).

155. "No weapon that is formed against you shall prosper" (Isa. 54:17).

PROMISE 16
YOU MAY ALL PROPHESY

156. "You may all prophesy" (1 Cor. 14:31).

157. God promised that in the last days He would pour out His Spirit on all flesh (Acts 2:17).

158. God promised that in the last days our sons and daughters would prophesy (Acts 2:17).

159. God promised that in the last days young men would see visions (Acts 2:17).

160. God promised that in the last days old men would dream dreams (Acts 2:17).

161. God promised that in the last days He would pour out His Spirit on His "menservants and maidservants" and "they shall prophesy" (Acts 2:18).

162. "The LORD will perfect that which concerns [us]" (Ps. 138:8, NKJV).

PROMISE 17
DREAMS FROM GOD

163. In dreams and visions of the night, when they sleep, God "opens the ears of men, and seals their instruction" (Job 33:15–16).

164. God promises to make Himself known to prophets in visions and dreams (Num. 12:6).

PROMISE 18
SIGNS AND WONDERS

165. God has chosen the children of God to manifest "signs" and "wonders" (Isa. 8:18).

166. "Jesus Christ is the same yesterday, and today, and forever" (Heb. 13:8).

167. The Father validates the Son by "miracles, wonders, and signs" (Acts 2:22, NKJV).

PROMISE 19
MOVING MOUNTAINS

168. Believers can move mountains (figuratively) with the spoken word (Mark 11:22–23).

169. The glory of the latter house will be greater than the glory of the former—on the highest level, prophetic of the church in the last days (Hag. 2:9).

170. Zerubbabel, governor of Judah, was promised that he would move the mountain of the enormous task of rebuilding the temple and that he would finish it shouting, "Grace! Grace," to it (Zech. 4:7).

171. God gave Zerubbabel a personal promise that we can all claim as well: "'Not by might nor by power, but by My Spirit,' says the LORD of hosts" (Zech. 4:6, NKJV).

172. When Jesus, the Messiah, came to this world, the Father promised, "Every valley shall be exalted" (Isa. 40:4, NKJV).

173. When Jesus, the Messiah, came to this world, the Father promised, "Every mountain and hill" shall be "brought low" (Isa. 40:4, NKJV).

174. When Jesus, the Messiah, came to this world, the Father promised, "The crooked places shall be made straight" (Isa. 40:4, NKJV).

175. When Jesus, the Messiah, came to this world, the Father promised, "The rough places" shall be made "smooth" (Isa. 40:4, NKJV).

176. "The glory of the LORD shall be revealed, and all flesh shall see it together" (Isa. 40:5).

177. If believers have "faith as a grain of mustard seed" then "nothing will be impossible" (Matt. 17:20).

178. Jesus said, "Whatever things you ask when you pray, believe that you will receive them, and you will have them" (Mark 11:24).

PROMISE 20
THE PROMISE OF THE FATHER

179. The baptism of the Holy Spirit is "the promise of the Father" (Acts 1:4–5).

180. When the Holy Spirit comes upon us, we "receive power" (Acts 1:8).

181. When the Holy Spirit comes upon us, we become Jesus's "witnesses" (Acts 1:8).

182. Those who repent and are baptized receive "forgiveness of sins" and "the gift of the Holy Spirit" (Acts 2:38).

183. Peter explained that this dual promise (forgiveness and the gift of the Holy Spirit) is "to you, and to your children, and to all who are far away, as many as the Lord our God will call" (Acts 2:39).

184. Jeremiah promised the coming of a new covenant in which the law would be written in the hearts of God's people, making them His people in a more profound sense (Jer. 31:33).

185. Jeremiah promised that all God's people in the new covenant would have a personal relationship with God and would know God (Jer. 31:34).

186. Jeremiah promised that in the new covenant God would forgive the iniquity of His people and "remember their sin no more" (Jer. 31:34).

187. Ezekiel promised a time would come when God would "cleanse" His people from their "filthiness" by sprinkling "clean water" on them—a symbolic reference to the Word and the Spirit (Ezek. 36:25).

188. God promised the time would come when He would give His people "a new heart" (Ezek. 36:26).

189. God promised the time would come when He would give His people "a new spirit" (Ezek. 36:26).

190. God promised the time would come when He would remove from His people a "stony heart" of prideful rebellion (Ezek. 36:26).

191. God promised the time would come when He would give His people "a heart of flesh" (a yielded, submissive, and sensitive heart, Ezek. 36:26).

192. Concerning the new covenant, God promised through Ezekiel, "I will put My Spirit within you" (Ezek. 36:27).

193. Concerning the new covenant, God promised through Ezekiel, "I will...cause you to walk in My statutes, and you will keep My judgments and do them" (Ezek. 36:27).

194. According to Joel, God promised that in the last days He would pour out His Spirit on all flesh and it would be a time of prophecy, visions, and dreams—a time when there would be "wonders" in the earth (Joel 2:28–30).

195. Malachi revealed that when the Messiah came, He would be like a refiner's fire and like launderers' soap, that He would purify His people (Mal. 3:2–3).

196. Malachi revealed that when the Messiah came, He would be "the Sun of Righteousness" arising with "healing in His wings" for those who "fear [His] name" (Mal. 4:2, NKJV).

197. When Jesus interceded over the church in John 17, He prayed that we would be kept from the evil one (John 17:15).

198. When Jesus interceded over the church in John 17, He prayed that we would all be sanctified by the truth (John 17:17).

199. When Jesus interceded over the church in John 17, He prayed that we would all receive the indwelling of the Son of God (John 17:26).

200. When Jesus interceded over the church in John 17, He prayed that we would be with Him where He is (John 17:24).

201. At that moment of salvation we are "sealed with the Holy Spirit of promise" (Eph. 1:13, NKJV).

202. We can each confess, "The Lord will deliver me from every evil work" (2 Tim. 4:18).

203. We can each confess, "The Lord...will preserve me for His heavenly kingdom, to whom be glory forever and ever. Amen" (2 Tim. 4:18).

Promise 21
Speaking in Tongues:
The Rest and the Refreshing

204. God foretold in the Old Testament era that He would speak to His people in "stammering lips and another tongue" (Isa. 28:11, NKJV).

205. God foretold that this supernatural manifestation would be "the rest" (Isa. 28:12, NKJV).

206. God foretold that this supernatural manifestation would be "the refreshing" (Isa. 28:12, NKJV).

207. When a person speaks in the "unknown tongue," in the spirit he "speaks mysteries" (1 Cor. 14:2).

208. When believers "pray in the Holy Spirit," they build themselves up in their "most holy faith" (Jude 20).

209. "The manifestation of the Spirit is given to everyone for the common good" (1 Cor. 12:7).

PROMISE 22
THE HEAD AND NOT THE TAIL

210. "The LORD will make you the head and not the tail" (Deut. 28:13).

211. "You will only be above and you will not be beneath" (Deut. 28:13).

212. The Lord chose Israel because He loved the Israelites and because He intended to keep His oath to the patriarchs (Deut. 7:6–8).

213. "He Himself bore our sins in His own body on the tree" (1 Pet. 2:24).

214. Jesus "redeemed us from the curse of the law" (Gal. 3:13).

215. Through the resurrection and ascension, the Father put "all things in subjection" under Jesus's feet (Eph. 1:22).

216. Jesus was made "head over all things for the church" (Eph. 1:22). This is a "headship exercised throughout the church" (Eph. 1:22, AMPC).

217. "When the enemy shall come in like a flood, the Spirit of the LORD shall lift up a standard against him" (Isa. 59:19).

218. He "always causes us to triumph in Christ" (2 Cor. 2:14).

PROMISE 23
METAMORPHOSIS

219. "But we all, seeing the glory of the Lord with unveiled faces, as in a mirror, are being transformed into the same image from glory to glory by the Spirit of the Lord" (2 Cor. 3:18).

220. Those foreknown of God "He predestined to be conformed to the image of His Son, so that He might be the firstborn among many brothers" (Rom. 8:29).

221. God declared His purpose in the beginning: "Let us make man in our image" (Gen. 1:26).

222. We are "transformed" by the "renewing" of our minds (Rom. 12:2).

223. This transformation enables us to discern "what is the good and acceptable and perfect will of God" (Rom. 12:2).

224. "We know that when He appears, we shall be like Him, for we shall see Him as He is" (1 John 3:2).

225. "For this corruptible will put on incorruption, and this mortal will put on immortality" (1 Cor. 15:53).

226. "When this corruptible will have put on incorruption, and this mortal will have put on immortality, then the saying that is written shall come to pass: 'Death is swallowed up in victory'" (1 Cor. 15:54).

PROMISE 24
MANSIONS IN HEAVEN—
OR SOMETHING FAR GREATER?

227. In the Father's "house" are "many mansions" (John 14:2, NKJV).

228. Jesus left this world to "prepare a place" for us (John 14:2).

229. If we love the Lord Jesus, the Father will love us (John 14:23).

230. Both the Father and the Son will come to that person who loves God and make their home with him or her (John 14:23).

231. Unimaginable and glorious things, which no eye has seen and no ear has heard, have been prepared by God for those who love Him (1 Cor. 2:9).

232. In the presence of the Lord His people experience "fullness of joy" (Ps. 16:11).

233. At the "right hand" of the Lord "there are pleasures for evermore" (Ps. 16:11).

PROMISE 25
THE FINAL PROMISE

234. Jesus said, "Surely I am coming soon" (Rev. 22:20).

235. "The Lord is not slack concerning His promise, as some count slackness, but is longsuffering toward us, not willing that any should perish but that all should come to repentance" (2 Pet. 3:9, NKJV).

236. Jesus will "descend from heaven with a shout" (1 Thess. 4:16).

237. Jesus will "descend from heaven...with the voice of the archangel" (1 Thess. 4:16).

238. Jesus will "descend from heaven...with the trumpet call of God," the sound of a heavenly shofar (1 Thess. 4:16).

239. Jesus will appear in "flaming fire" (2 Thess. 1:7–8).

240. Jesus will appear with all His holy angels (Matt. 25:31).

241. In the day of His coming, "the light of the moon shall be as the light of the sun, and the light of the sun shall be sevenfold, as the light of seven days" (Isa. 30:26).

242. The "veil" of flesh-consciousness "spread over all nations" will be destroyed (Isa. 25:7).

243. "The dead in Christ will rise first" (1 Thess. 4:16).

244. "Then we who are alive and remain shall be caught up together with them in the clouds to meet the Lord in the air" (1 Thess. 4:17).

245. "And so we shall be forever with the Lord" (1 Thess. 4:17).

246. "We shall all be changed. In a moment, in the twinkling of an eye" (1 Cor. 15:51–52).

247. When the Son of God descends, "His feet will stand on the Mount of Olives," and it will be "split in two halves by a very great valley" (Zech. 14:4).

248. The Antichrist (the "lawless one") will be destroyed by the Lord, by "the brightness of His presence" (2 Thess. 2:8).

249. "The kings of the earth with their armies" will be conquered by the Lord in the last days (Rev. 19:19).

250. "The kingdom and dominion, and the greatness of all the kingdoms under the whole heaven, shall be given to the people of the saints of the Most High" (Dan. 7:27).

251. "The meek" will "inherit the earth" (Matt. 5:5).

252. We will finally "see His face" (Rev. 22:4).

253. "Living water will flow out from Jerusalem" (Zech. 14:8).

254. The Messiah "shall judge among the nations, and shall rebuke many peoples" (Isa. 2:4).

255. The people of this world will "beat their swords into plowshares, and their spears into pruning hooks" (Isa. 2:4).

256. "Nation shall not lift up sword against nation, nor shall they learn war any more" (Isa. 2:4).

257. "The wolf and the lamb shall feed together, and the lion shall eat straw like the bull (Isa. 65:25).

258. "They shall not hurt nor destroy in all My holy mountain, says the Lord" (Isa. 65:25).

259. The redeemed of the Lord will be "kings and priests unto our God; and we shall reign on the earth" (Rev. 5:10).

260. An angel will bind Satan in a "bottomless pit" (Rev. 20:1–3).

261. Jesus "will transform our body of humiliation, so that it may be conformed to His glorious body" (Phil. 3:21).

262. We will be like Jesus in appearance. He is the "sun of righteousness" (Mal. 4:2). In the day of resurrection "the righteous will shine forth as the sun in the kingdom of their Father" (Matt. 13:43).

263. We will be like Jesus in authority. "All things" are "under His feet" (Eph. 1:22). Also, the Scripture says of God's people, "What is man that You are mindful of him, and the son of man that You attend to him? For You have made him a little lower than the angels, and crowned him with glory and honor. You have given him dominion over the works of Your hands; You have put all things under his feet" (Ps. 8:4–6).

264. We will be like Jesus in intelligence. "For now we see as through a glass, dimly, but then, face to face. Now I know in part, but then I shall know, even as I also am known" (1 Cor. 13:12).

265. We will be like Jesus in emotions. He said, "My peace I give to you" (John 14:27).

266. We will be like Jesus in emotions. He said, "…that My joy may remain in you" (John 15:11).

267. We will be like Jesus in emotions. He prayed to the Father for all His disciples, "that the love with which You loved Me may be in them" (John 17:26).

268. We will be like Jesus in supernatural abilities and works. "Truly, truly I say to you, he who believes in Me will do the works that I do also. And he will do greater works than these, because I am going to My Father" (John 14:12).

269. We will be like Jesus in oneness with the Father. "...that they may all be one, as You, Father, are in Me, and I in You. May they also be one in Us, that the world may believe that You have sent Me" (John 17:21).

270. We will be like Jesus in glory. "I have given them the glory which You gave Me, that they may be one even as We are one" (John 17:22).

271. We will be like Jesus in holiness. "Just as He chose us in Him before the foundation of the world, to be holy and blameless before Him in love" (Eph. 1:4).

272. We will be like Jesus in perfection. "I in them, and You in Me; that they may be made perfect in one" (John 17:23, NKJV; see also Col. 1:28). The scripture for *unchangeableness* is included as number 289 (Rev. 3:12).

273. God will express Himself fully in every child of God, "that God may be all in all" (1 Cor. 15:28).

274. The "whole creation groans and travails in pain together until now" (like a mother in labor), anticipating the full manifestation of the sons of God (Rom. 8:22).

275. "Because the creation itself also will be delivered from the bondage of corruption into the glorious liberty of the children of God" (Rom. 8:21, NKJV).

276. "The heavens will be dissolved, being on fire, and the elements will melt with fervent heat" (2 Pet. 3:12, NKJV).

277. "Nevertheless we, according to His promise, look for new heavens and a new earth in which righteousness dwells" (2 Pet. 3:13, NKJV).

278. When Jesus comes, His reward is with Him "to give to each one according to his work" (Rev. 22:12).

279. Those who overcome will "eat of the tree of life, which is in the midst of the Paradise of God" (Rev. 2:7).

280. Those who are faithful unto death will receive a "crown of life" (Rev. 2:10).

281. Those who overcome "shall not be hurt by the second death" (Rev. 2:11).

282. Those who overcome will be given "the hidden manna to eat" (Rev. 2:17).

283. Those who overcome will be given "a white stone, and on the stone a new name written, which no one knows except he who receives it" (Rev. 2:17).

284. Those who overcome and keep God's works until the end will be given "authority over the nations" (Rev. 2:26).

285. Those who overcome will be given "the morning star," which probably means a new beginning eternally in Christ (Rev. 2:28).

286. Those who overcome will be "clothed in white garments" (Rev. 3:5).

287. Those who overcome will not have their names blotted out of the Book of Life (Rev. 3:5).

288. Those who overcome will have the Son of God confess their names before the Father and His angels (Rev. 3:5).

289. Those who overcome will be made pillars in the temple of God and will never go out again (Rev. 3:12).

290. Those who overcome and become pillars in the temple of God will receive the signature of God upon their existence forever—as Jesus said, "I will write on him the name of My God and the name of the city of My God, the New Jerusalem, which comes down out of heaven from My God, and My own new name" (Rev. 3:12).

291. Those who overcome will be enthroned with the Lord forever, sharing the reins of the new creation (Rev. 3:21; this promise was also shared in promise 3 but emphasizing our authority right now, so it is repeated here in an eternal sense).

292. Those who overcome "shall inherit all things" (Rev. 21:7).

293. Those who overcome will enjoy a sonship relationship with the Father of creation forever (Rev. 21:7).

294. We are destined for a celestial city (New Jerusalem) "which has foundations, whose builder and maker is God" (Heb. 11:10).

295. "This is the promise that He has promised us—eternal life" (1 John 2:25).

CONCLUSION
PRAYING THE PROMISES

296. "Those who wait upon the LORD shall renew their strength" (Isa. 40:31).

297. "Those who wait upon the LORD...mount up with wings as eagles" (Isa. 40:31).

298. "Those who wait upon the LORD...shall run and not be weary" (Isa. 40:31).

299. "Those who wait upon the LORD...shall walk and not faint" (Isa. 40:31).

300. Jesus promised, "If you ask anything in My name, I will do it" (John 14:14).

NOTES

EPIGRAPH

1. "Dwight L. Moody Quotes," BrainyQuote, accessed February 7, 2018, https://www.brainyquote.com/quotes/dwight_l _moody_157634.

CHAPTER 1
PROMISES, PROMISES—AND ALL OF THEM TRUE!

1. Herbert Lockyer, *All the Promises of the Bible* (Grand Rapids, MI: Lamplighter Books, Zondervan Publishing Company, 1962), 10.

CHAPTER 3
PATRIARCH OF THE PROMISES

1. "The Church Moved by the Hand of God," Economic Development Partnership of North Carolina, accessed March 8, 2018, https://www.visitnc.com/listing/the-church-moved-by -the-hand-of-god.

2. Rick Schwartz, *Hurricanes and the Middle Atlantic States* (Blue Diamond Books, 2007), accessed March 8, 2018, http:// www.snopes.com/religion/floatingchurch.asp.

3. "The Church Moved by the Hand of God," *Carolina Weekly*, accessed March 8, 2018, www.carolinaweeklynews.com /id89.html.

CHAPTER 5
RECEIVING A NEW IDENTITY

1. The author has written a Charisma House book titled *Who Am I?: Dynamic Declarations of Who You Are in Christ*, which explores fifty-two of our God-given names and titles. There are over one thousand given to God's people in the Bible.

Learning them imparts a grand panoramic view of who we are and what we possess as children of the Highest.

PROMISE 4
THE HUNDREDFOLD RETURN

1. "Jim Elliot," Wikipedia, accessed March 12, 2018, https://en.wikipedia.org/wiki/Jim_Elliot.

PROMISE 19
MOVING MOUNTAINS

1. You can read the entire story of this amazing miracle with documentation from medical reports and X-rays in Ben Godwin's book *God's Strategy for Tragedy* (Cleveland, TN: Deeper Revelation Books, 2008).

CONCLUSION
PRAYING THE PROMISES

1. "Kenneth E. Hagin Quotes," Goodreads, accessed March 14, 2018, https://www.goodreads.com/quotes/972904-you-are-what-you-read.

2. Kenneth E. Hagin, "Possessing the Promise of Healing," Kenneth Hagin Ministries, accessed March 14, 2018, http://www.rhema.org/index.php?option=com_content&view=article&id=232:possessing-the-promise-of-healing&Itemid=144.